SAGGISTICA 18

Rope and Soap
Lynchings of Italians in the United States

Rope and Soap
Lynchings of Italians in the United States

Patrizia Salvetti

Translated from the Italian by
Fabio Girelli-Carasi

BORDIGHERA PRESS

Library of Congress Control Number: 2015959520

Cover image:

LAW RESUMES ITS SWAY
The Illustrated American
4 April 1891

Originally published in Italian as

Corda e sapone: storie dei linciaggi di Italiani negli USA
Donzelli, 2012

© 2017 translation Fabio Girelli-Carasi
© 2012 Italian version by Donizelli Editore

All rights reserved. Parts of this book may be reprinted only by written permission from the author, and may not be reproduced for publication in book, magazine, or electronic media of any kind, except for purposes of literary reviews by critics.

Printed in the United States.

Published by
BORDIGHERA PRESS
John D. Calandra Italian American Institute
25 West 43rd Street, 17th Floor
New York, NY 10036

SAGGISTICA 18
ISBN 978-1-59954-101-3

TABLE OF CONTENTS

Introduction to the English Version (vii)
    Fabio Girelli-Carasi

Translator's Note (xiii)

ROPE AND SOAP

Foreword (xvii)

Introduction (3)

1. The Beginning of Impunity (37)

2. The Great Lynching and the False Lynching (47)

3. Not Only the South: In the West (81)

4. In the Old South (91)

5. When Law Enforcement Acts: Nine Potential Lynchings That Did Not Happen (135)

6. The Last Lynching of Italians (147)

7. America Interrogates Itself (167)

Index of Names (181)

Introduction to the English Translation
Fabio Girelli-Carasi

The extraordinary documentary value of Patrizia Salvetti's research is so evident that it makes it almost redundant to label it "a seminal study." I don't think anyone will doubt that this work will open new horizons and an entire new field of inquiry for scholars interested in the phenomenon of Italian immigration to the United States — in its entirety and from several different perspectives: not only history, but anthropology, cultural studies, political science, and even constitutional law.

Every page is full to the rim with new information based on primary sources, accurately referenced to documents contemporary of those horrifying events that go under the name of lynchings.

Borrowing an expression from another realm of academic inquiry, the readers will confidently conclude that this research is the equivalent of "basic science," the kind of discovery that is bound to propel the discipline in a new direction while contributing to the multifaceted debate on the relation between Italy and her daughters and sons who were forced to leave.

A few aspects of the phenomenon of lynchings of Italians in the United States are already known, at least in specialized circles. Among researchers on Italian American studies the most gruesome episodes had already been documented and investigated, although not completely digested. First among them was the largest mass lynching ever perpetrated on American soil, the infamous massacre of 13 individuals of Italian descent in New Orleans in 1891, an atrocity that saw the complicity of the press and the explicit approval of the city's "prominents."

An even smaller group of scholars is also acquainted with the Tampa lynching of 1910, although the notoriety of the events probably owes more to the context in which they occurred: the struggle by labor unions against what today we call "management" and which Italians, then and now, simply call "i padroni."

Patrizia Salvetti's study, however, is not simply a catalog of racist crimes committed against Italian citizens of recently naturalized U.S. nationals who had left "the Old Country" both to conquer a dream and to escape a nightmare. This book tells us why and how those lynchings were committed, it connects them to the broader topic of white power and white dominance, how it was enforced and maintained in a large portion of the country. It also tells us that lynching was applied to Italians as a special treatment sanctioned by political motives that found in racism their alibi. It also tells us, most damning to the eternally distracted Italian consular institutions – what could have been done to prevent the repeating and the spreading of those barbarous acts beyond the boundaries of some dark corners of the Deep South into sunny new frontiers from Florida to Colorado and as far north as Pennsylvania.

Salvetti's work has dug deeply into the mother lode of official correspondence between the Italian government all the way up to the office of the prime minister via the Ministry of Foreign Affairs (Ministero Affari Esteri — MAE) and the Italian diplomatic corps and its effort to offer a modicum of protection to their citizens by pressing the counterparts in the U.S. Department of State. For Italian Americans, accustomed and inured to the culture of paternalistic neglect dispensed by Italian diplomats in this country (no need to expand on the topic here), it will be both of comfort and surprise to discover that in several circumstances the agents of the Italian government present in America took to heart the tragedies they were witnessing with increased frequency in the territories of their pertinence. Some of them were courageous and forceful in advocating for the community and in advancing demands of vigorous investigation, prosecution and punishment of the killers and their associates. At times they became deeply involved on an emotional level, outraged at what they saw as an atmosphere of unqualified brutality and the unbridled exercise of ruthless power by the authorities in charge. More than the crime, in fact, it was the impenetrable blanket of *omertà* by American authorities that inflamed and offended Italian consular agents — *omertà* that inevitably led to systematic cover-ups of evidence and resulted in impunity for the perpetrators and instigators of the crimes.

One of these agents, Pasquale Corte, consul in New Orleans at the time of the infamous mass massacre, was so explicit in his condemnation of the American justice system that he put his own career at stake and was recalled to Italy by the minister for his excessive zeal (page 63).

As the consulate staffers did what they could — with some significant exceptions, of course — the Rome-based institutions, government and ministries, responded rather phlegmatically and, it seems, without the sense of urgency that the circumstances warranted. At the core of the dispute between Italy and the United States were not simply truculent murders of Italian citizens for which no one had ever been found guilty. The episodes of lynching were not part of the random cases of violence that ended up with the murders of Italians unrelated to their identity. The so-called "people's justice" targeted Italians for the same reason it also victimized African Americans, Chinese and Mexicans, because they represented a threat to the power establishment. It was a terroristic message: Strike one to terrorize all.

The fact that the local authorities were conniving and at times directly involved challenged the core of the international treaty signed by Italy and the United States about the protection of their citizens on the respective foreign soil. Italians were guaranteed by the signature of the president and the ratification of the Senate that they would enjoy the same rights and protection under the law that were granted to Americans. However, the federal government refused to take an active part in the investigation and prosecution of these heinous crimes on the basis of the constitutional doctrine of state rights, whereby these crimes fell within the jurisdiction of the individual states while the federal government had no power to intervene.

This caused enormous frustration on the part of Italian institutions, or at least on the part of the individuals most committed to the principles of justice, human rights and respect of sovereign dignity. At the same time, the sophistry of the argument put forth by the state department gave an excuse to the less committed, both in Italy and in the United States, to simply bypass the thorny and complex issue of relations between states and head straight for a palliative solution. Every lynching would result in impunity for the culprit and a monetary compensation for the descendants of the victims. The president would propose and Congress would approve such compensations under the guise of an act of mercy, without ever admitting that they were meant as settlement for damages. In short, charity.

The Italian language press exploded with indignation every time the Italian government accepted this "blood money." Frustration and humiliation merged together with increasing fear that the *de facto* impunity for the culprits would contribute to the spreading of crimes against Italians. And for a while, in particular in the first decade of the twentieth century, this prophecy seemed correct.

But Salvetti's book doesn't simply report how Italian institutions failed their citizens in America. Quite evenhandedly, it reports on the long, complex and extremely well-articulated strategy devised by Ambassador Saverio Fava to solve the constitutional contradiction that the American government in theory guaranteed certain rights to Italians and other foreigners, while in practice could do nothing to enforce them. Individual states were free to deny them at will. (The default argument by the State Department was that Italians indeed enjoyed the same protection as American citizens. After all, the states treated lynchings of Italians the same way they handled the lynchings of Americans, namely, they did nothing.)

Ambassador Fava was supported in his effort by an American public and a media that, after decades of carnage, had become sickened by this practice. Also on his side was a growing number of politicians in the House and the Senate. Finally, President McKinley, firmly on the side of allowing more immigrants into the country, threw his support behind this project to rein in at least in part the horror of lynching.

A bill was finally introduced in the Senate: its provisions would transfer the jurisdiction for lynchings away from local authorities and assign it to the federal government. Federal agents with no connections to the local authorities where crimes were committed would investigate, and federal magistrates would prosecute and try the cases. An important aspect of this legislation was the novel and ingenious device that would safeguard state rights while allowing the federal government to have a role in the administration of justice. The federal magistrates, in fact, would prosecute the cases not according to federal statutes, but using the laws of the state where the crime had been committed.

Whether this audacious project had a real chance of passing, given the intransigent opposition of a large block of votes from the South and the West, will never be known. President McKinley was assassinated in 1901, paradoxically by an immigrant, and the momentum behind the legislative effort quickly dissolved. The progresses made on the bill, approved in the Senate Judiciary Committee, became null when the legislature expired and a new Congress was elected. Moreover, the last nail in the coffin was the election to the presidency of Theodore Roosevelt, who turned out to be, if not outright hostile to the bill, at least indifferent.

Thus vanished the dream of affecting a constitutional change that — undoubtedly — in the long term would have changed the history of America for the better. What Italians were left with were small sums of "blood money," a wounded pride and an uncertain future ahead.

Translator's Note

Translating Patrizia Salvetti's Italian prose is a breeze. Clarity, precision and a smooth style make the text not just readable but truly enjoyable.

Quite a different endeavor, however, is the translation of the prose of Italian diplomats and politicians who are abundantly quoted in the book. With a few exceptions, the correspondence between various officers, reports, analyses and situational assessments are written in the "high prose" of traditional rhetoric, informed primarily by the study of classical languages and in particular Latin.

The benchmark of eloquence and elegance for this crowd was the "periodo ciceroniano," or "Cicero's turn-of-phrase": paragraph-long sentences, dense with subordinate, parenthetical and incidental clauses, supported by an intricate syntax made of anaphoric references (both backward and forward anaphora).

This was the training that Italian schools, Liceo Classico in particular, imparted to the privileged élite that constituted the diplomatic corps (mostly from aristocratic families). This is how they were taught to write.

Italian language can afford to do so (but English has come close to this complexity in the works of genius David Foster Wallace) thanks to its morphological density. The plasticity of the Italian sentence structure allows the reordering at will of the standard string of Subject Verb Object to produce nuances and effects embedded in alternative word orders. This would not be possible in the absence of morphological rails that keep the discourse on track: subject-verb agreement directs the reader to properly assign meaning to complex constructions. Moreover, nouns and adjectives and their correlate pronouns carry gender markers (masculine-feminine) and number markers (singular-plural) that guide comprehension through thick webs of internal references.

Last but not least, the use of verb moods such as the subjunctive and conditional allow nuances of meaning that, in an English translation, require the language to resort to additional intrusive adverbs and periphrases to capture the tone and mark the distance between the writer and the opinion being expressed.

In order to translate this flow of words I had two choices. The first was to chop up every phrase into small pieces, each conveying a single unit of message. This would have resulted in infinite repetitions of words and concepts, like a chain in which each short sentence worked as a link between the preceding and the following link -- flat and atonal.

The second choice was to attempt to reproduce the multilayered structure of the "periodo ciceroniano" and its basic scaffold, with as few breaks as possible so as to avoid repetition of words and concepts. I chose this second strategy, mindful that the text deviates from the standard expository style of English. As such in certain points it will require a greater degree of attention by the reader. I am, however, confident that the surrounding prose by Patrizia Salvetti and the powerful messages embedded in her arguments will easily compensate for the effort required to read a few lines of century-old bureaucratic prose.

Rope and Soap
Lynchings of Italians in the United States

Patrizia Salvetti

Foreword

In the course of my ongoing research on Italian emigrants to the Americas, in 1999 I began to focus my attention on the lynching of Italians in the United States. I immediately discovered that the history of those episodes was basically unknown both to my Italian colleagues and to American scholars of contemporary history with the sole exception of few experts on Italian migration to the United States.

That is not to say that the frequent cases of mistreatment of Italian emigrants have not been studied and analyzed. Indeed, abuses and violence against Italians in the United States between the end of the nineteenth and the beginning of the twentieth centuries are well documented. The same is also true for the discrimination suffered by Italians in Latin America and Australia and the frequent episodes of violent xenophobia that targeted them in Europe, in particular in France and Switzerland.[1]

There was, however, a major dark hole in the history of lynching of Italians and in the research of Italian as well as American historians. This runs contrary to the notoriety of cases with a clear political connotation, such as the Sacco and Vanzetti trials, that is well known beyond the circles of experts. In the United States numerous studies have tackled the phenomenon of lynching, with analyses of its symbolic meaning, its geographical and temporal coordinates and the struggle to stamp out such an abominable practice. However, American historians who have studied this phenomenon have focused most of their attention on the lynching of African Americans,[2] its racial aspects, rationale and semiotic meaning.

---

[1] For a reconstruction of some of the episodes of discrimination and mistreatment suffered by Italians in Europe, the Americas and Australia, see G. A. Stella, *L'orda. Quando gli albanesi eravamo noi*. Milano: Rizzoli, 2002.

[2] A chronology of lynchings in the United States claiming to be the most complete account was published in 1991. Only three cases of lynchings of Italians are listed (New Orleans, Tallulah, Tampa). It erroneously includes an episode near Seattle in

They have, though, widely underestimated, both in terms of quantity and quality, the lynching of other non-black ethnic groups and in particular Italians. I noticed the same attitude in the reports of Italian diplomats kept in the archives of the Italian Ministry of Foreign Affairs — one of the major sources for my research. In discussing the lynching of Italians, the diplomats had the tendency to "forget" some of them and to report only the most grievous cases, or those that had caused complex diplomatic incidents.[3] I noticed that the image of lynching very often coincided with the narrative of the "frontier justice" in the period when the West was first invaded and colonized by white settlers — the period that was made popular by western movies. A second narrative focused on the Deep South and the hangings of black people by the white establishment in situations of economic and cultural backwardness and a radical attachment to old traditions. It was, however, shocking to discover that even royal subjects of His Majesty the King of Italy could be the targets of such brutal practices. In addition, such a high number of victims was also stunning. Although the thirty-four Italian victims — plus another dozen saved at the last minute — were an infinitesimal fraction of the number of black lynchings, they were the first ethnic group after blacks and Chinese.

1892 that in reality did not take place. See Michael Newton and Judy Ann Newton, *Racial & Religious Violence in America: A Chronology.* New York-London: Newton, 1991.

[3] In order to reconstruct the context in which the lynchings of Italians in the United States took place starting in the last two decades of the nineteenth century, I used the documents held in the historical-diplomatic archive of the Ministry of Foreign Affairs (ASDMAE). These documents contain a wealth of information on all sorts of subjects, and in particular secret reports sent by the embassy to the various ministers summarizing reports by consuls: they contain news, private conversations and observations typically omitted in official documents. These sources alone, however, could not provide sufficient information on the political, social and economic situation in which the lynchings took place. For that I had to turn to other sources in order to get a larger picture of the American and Italian public opinion. Among others, I investigated the Italian-language press in the United States, the local English-language press, Italian parliamentary records and documents of the Foreign Relations of the United States (FRUS).

In 2000 the New York Historical Society organized a courageous exhibit about lynching in the United States under the title *Without Sanctuary*, with the display of a tragic collection of photographs and postcards depicting men, primarily African Americans, who had been burned, mutilated, hanged or tortured: all this, in front of crowds of "normal" people.

The collection narrated a long chapter of American history, primarily from the 1880s to the 1920s. Under the guise of a calm normality, this was the history of a wave of collective assassinations, which reached a peak at the turn of the century.

The catalogue[4] included only two photos of a lynching of Italians in Tampa, Florida, in 1910. There were also photos of episodes involving other ethnic groups and white people, although, quite appropriately, the majority of images represented African Americans, by far the largest group of American citizens subjected to this practice. And yet, even with such limited evidence, I noticed that my colleagues were surprised to find out in that exhibit that two Italians were among the victims of lynching. Once more I realized how little the world knew about that aspect of emigration, full of mistreatment, abuses, discrimination and violence suffered by so many Italian emigrants and so easily ignored in favor of the success of a few.

In my work, far from facing the theme of lynching in its complexity, I limited my analysis to the episodes that involved Italian citizens in the United States between the end of the nineteenth century and the first two decades of the twentieth and to the reactions of the Italian government through its official representatives in Washington. I also decided to include the cases when lynching was avoided; namely, cases where local authorities or the National Guard sent by governors arrived just in time to prevent an impending massacre. When a lynching did take place, the assumption must be that law enforcement and public order forces were standing by or, worse, were directly complicit in the misdeed. Included

---

[4] J. Allen, ed. *Without Sanctuary. Lynching Photography in America.* Santa Fe: Twin Palms Publishers, 2000. The exhibit triggered a wide Internet debate in the United States. See A. Lorini "Cartoline dall'inferno. Storia e memoria pubblica dei linciaggi negli Stati Uniti" in *Passato e Presente* 55 January-April 2002, 129-35.

in my analysis is also the case of a fake case of lynching of Italians in Seattle, Washington, in 1892. Not only was the act never carried out, but it was not even planned. Both the American press and the Italian consul for days[5] tried to find out what had happened: this episode seems indicative of the climate of suspicion and fear that had spread after the New Orleans lynchings of 1891. I also added to the list those episodes that resulted in the *de facto* lynching[6] of Italians, although they cannot formally be assigned to the category. They are, as Ambassador Edmondo Mayor des Planches commented, collective murders with "some elements of lynching." And finally, I chose to group in my study episodes that involved Italians who had been naturalized as American citizens, and, therefore, cases in which the Italian embassy could not intervene. The lynching party could not possibly know if and when an Italian had acquired American nationality. To them, they were just lynching an Italian who deserved it.

---

[5] See ASDMAE, Serie Politica "P", b. 357. See also *Seattle Press-Times.* June 13-27, 1892.
[6] ASDMAE, Serie Politica "P" (1891-1916), b. 683. From the Italian Embassy, Washington, to the Ministry of Foreign Affairs (MAE), June 29, 1903.

Rope and Soap

INTRODUCTION

1. Lynching in the History of the United States: A National Crime?

What do we mean when we use the term "lynching"? And what is the origin of the term itself? These are questions that the field of historical studies in the United States[1] has not yet put to definite rest. Even the etymology of the word is still being debated. Among various possibilities, the hypothesis most often mentioned and found in most encyclopedias traces the origin to the name of Colonel Charles Lynch, a prominent Quaker from Bedford County, Virginia. In the Colonial period toward the end of the eighteenth century, during the American Revolution, Lynch started administering summary justice to rustlers who sold stolen horses to the British army. The closest courthouse was in Williamsburg, about 200 miles from Bedford County, too far for the community's demand for swift and effective justice. In these circumstances, by general consensus, Lynch's house was chosen to function as courthouse with the colonel appointed judge, assisted by three advisers.

In 1782, after the end of the revolution, the state of Virginia ratified this arrangement and promulgated "Lynch's Law," giving Lynch and his advisers immunity from penal and civil prosecution, whence derived the association of Lynch-the-person with the practice of *lynching*. It goes without saying that in the United States there had been countless episodes of summary justice, with various names and definitions, even before the practice of Lynch's Law spread around the country.

The Virginia law was the only example of jurisprudence that officially established for lynching a specific legal definition. As new waves of

---

[1] See J. E. Cutler. *Lynching-Law: An Investigation into the History of Lynching in the United States.* New York: New York, Longmans, Green, and Co., 1905.

immigration swarmed toward the West, this extra-legal method of summary justice spread and became a national practice of social defense that lasted into the twentieth century.

Beyond the historical and linguistic origins, the practice of lynching has distinct and peculiar properties that separate it from other forms of collective murder, including those perpetrated by secret societies like the Ku Klux Klan.[2] Lynching came in various forms that differed greatly depending on the time and location where it was administered. Among the variables were the number of people involved in the lynching party, ranging from a few dozens to several thousands; the organizational set-up; the method of killing; the reason and the kind of crime for which the punishment was meted out. All of the episodes, however, shared certain characteristics: first was mob violence that culminated in the capture of suspects of certain crimes, followed by the observance of a ceremonial ritual in front of the mob. Usually, but not necessarily in every case, the mob forcibly removed the suspects from the jail where they were incarcerated and dragged them to a location in the open. The only exceptions were a few cases when the execution took place in the jail itself. "Taken from legal custody" was the legal definition of the kidnappings. The formula was applied to excuse the local authorities responsible for the lack of protection of the prisoners.

One of the most striking aspects present in every case was the composition of the lynching party. This was not a mob of deviant characters beyond the boundaries of society. Quite the contrary: on an individual

---

[2] The Ku Klux Klan was founded by a group of Confederate soldiers in Tennessee in 1866 after the end of the Civil War. At the beginning it was supposed to be a secret society with recreational purposes. Following a period of political, social and economic crisis in the southern states, it quickly became a secret society with the "mission" of defending social order and preserving the purity of the white Anglo-Saxon race, and as such it began to spread to other states in the South. The cult of violence mixed with the racist ideology led the KKK and other similar secret societies to commit all sorts of killings following specific rituals. The victims were mostly black people with no pretense that they were chosen for their criminal activities. Starting in 1870, the Ku Klux Klan was investigated by the federal government. It ostensibly dissolved itself but was later reconstituted in 1915.

level they were "good and honest" citizens, perfectly integrated into society, who felt the duty to defend the value of justice and the traditions of American civilization by inflicting cruel but necessary exemplary punishments. At the end of the nineteenth century, an erudite Italian traveler, Giovanni De Riseis, who, incidentally, had very little sympathy for immigrants he met in Colorado (he described then as "knife-wielding drunkards" and "ugly characters"), described the psychological mechanism at work in an individual in the moment when he surrenders his judgment to the rule of the mob. Concerning the lynching of an Italian in Denver in 1893, he reported that the lynchers were model citizens: "However, when many meek and friendly people gather together, soon they turn into mobs of violent lynchers.[3] When people are absolutely convinced of their own righteousness and they decide to inflict violence not for the sake of violence itself or for personal retribution, but in order to uphold a higher principle, they feel collectively absolved by the mob they are part of. This renders violence acceptable in moral and social terms when it is applied to other people who are seen as being on the outside of their system of rules."

2. The Mob

Crowds are always described as *mobs* by official reports and the press. In comparison to the word *crowd* that has rather neutral connotations, *mob* stands to indicate an unruly and potentially aggressive gathering of people. Until the 1880s lynchings usually took place at night, carried out by groups of masked people. Beginning in the 1890s lynchings became more and more public affairs with a choreographic and spectacular component. The participants no longer covered their faces, thus claiming the legitimacy of their actions and the symbolic value of their participation in a ritual that, in most cases, did not stop at the execution without trial, but was accompanied by ritual torture before and after death. Often the dead body was left exposed for viewing for several

---

[3] Giovanni De Riseis. *Dagli Stati Uniti alle Indie*. Roma: Raimondi e Colombo, 1899.

hours and the images were reproduced in photographs and even postcards. Quite often the local newspapers, which could be openly or quietly complicit, announced in advance the time and place of the shows that were attended by entire families, children included, as at a town's picnic. The main aspect that characterized lynching was the certainty of impunity for the crime, fruit of the sort of "people's justice" that was socially acceptable and was *de facto* not prosecuted by the official organs of justice. It was common practice for the magistrate to file charges against unknown individuals and for trials to end with a guilty verdict. The names of the culprits, of course, were indeed very well known to all.

The tradition of lynching is certainly characteristic of the United States. However, it is also true that precedents can be found in other parts of the world. Executions similar to lynchings, when the "people's justice" replaced formal justice, belong to the history of humanity from antiquity to the Middle Ages to the absolute monarchy period until it became progressively more rare in recent times. For instance, in the storming of the Bastille, which lit the powders of the French Revolution, people's sovereignty replaced the power establishment and led to all sorts of massacres in the name of "people's justice."[4] There are, however, very few analogies between these events and the essence of "American-style" lynching, mostly because in America the "political" dimension of violence was missing. Also missing was the notion of the replacement of a form of power with a new one.

History reports a large number of xenophobic violent episodes against Italian emigrants around the world, mainly in France, some of which culminated in brutal rioting and crowd violence with a tragically large count of victims, the most notorious of which was the massacre at Aigues-Mortes, in the Camargue, a region of southern France, where in 1883 a large number of Italians who were competing with the locals for

---

[4] Mob violence in the French Revolution has been discussed extensively in scholarly literature according to different approaches such as historical studies, psychoanalysis and anthropology. See R. Cobb. *Polizia e popolo. La protesta popolare in Francia (1789-1820)*. Bologna: Il Mulino, 1976.

scarce jobs in the salinas were killed by a mob.[5] Yet, even these cases were substantially different from the cases of lynching. Episodes of lynching took place in Italy during and immediately after World War II. The most notorious was that of Donato Carretta, warden of Regina Coeli, Rome's main prison, in September 1944. Still, there are very few similarities between these and the American cases based on Lynch's Law in which violence was not directed at symbols of power and therefore lacked a "political" component.[6] All things considered, it can be argued that lynching is not part of the history and traditions of Italy and Europe.

Count Gerolamo Moroni, in charge of immigration at the Italian consulate in New Orleans, handled the case of lynching of two Italians in Tampa, Florida, in 1910. Initially, rumors were circulating that the two were victims of internal contrasts within the Italian colony. He aptly observed and sarcastically commented that: "Lynching is a type of crime that Italians have not mastered yet. It's possible that someday our immigrants will learn it from the civilized Americans."[7] Moreover, "American-style" lynchings were usually premeditated and organized. They were not just an explosion of uncontrolled rage on the part of a crowd. In order to give an exemplary lesson it was important to show a degree of "professionalism" and preparation that was totally absent in the lynching episodes or spontaneous outbursts of violence outside the United States. At the same time, it would be incorrect to reduce "American-style" lynching to some sort of private vendetta, where a group of citizens punished an enemy of the community as retaliation against a grievous offense. The act was performed in the name of the community, in defense of the community itself and its violated values. The community performed this

---

[5] See E. Barnabà. *Morte agli italiani. Il massacro di Aigues-Mortes.* Giardini Naxos: Infinito, 2001.
[6] An exhaustive reconstruction of the episode is in G. Ranzato. *Il linciaggio di Carretta. Roma 1944: violenza politica e ordinaria violenza.* Milano: Il Saggiatore, 1977.
[7] ASDMAE, Serie "Z," Usa, b. 33, f. 27/2. From the Consulate of Italy in New Orleans to MAE, October 8, 1910.

act of justice following an established ritual needed to ennoble cruelty against those who broke the common moral and social code.

3. A SOUTHERN OBSESSION?

Lynching as a semi-legal institution was often defined as a national crime. In this sense it belongs to the history and traditions of the United States. Mark Twain, with unique sarcasm, called the nation "the United States of Lyncherdom." In reality the practice can be better defined as a Southern obsession, an integral part of the culture of the states of the Deep South.[8] One of the less-credible hypotheses that attempted to explain why the South was the primary — albeit not the exclusive — region where lynching took place claimed a direct correlation with the warmer climate. According to this thesis, it was the heat of summer months that caused a higher frequency of lynchings. In a report to the Minister of Foreign Affairs Tommaso Tittoni, in 1905 the Italian Ambassador in Washington, Edmondo Mayor des Planches, wrote: "Every year summer marks an increase in lynching."[9] A more plausible reason for the increase in June and July points to the fact that tighter control was needed in this period of the year when agricultural production reached its peak and social tensions between white land owners and black labor also escalated. "Punishment" of black people was therefore used as a deterrent.[10] Ambassador Mayor de Planches believed that lynching was not tied to the culture of the South but simply to a higher concentration of black people in those states. In a report to Minister

---

[8] W.F. Brundage. *Lynching in the New South, Georgia and Virginia, 1880-1930*. Urbana-Chicago: University of Illinois Press, 1993; R. P. Ingalls. *Urban Vigilantes in the New South: Tampa 1882-1936*. Knoxville: University of Tennessee Press, 1988; E.L. Ayers. *The Promise of the New South*. New York: Oxford University Press, 1992; J. Higham. *Strangers in the Land: Patterns of American Nativism (1860-1925)*. Westport, Conn. : Greenwood Press, 1981, c1963; P. Dray. *At the Hands of Persons Unknown: the Lynching of Black America*. New York: Modern Library, 2003; E.M. Back, S.E. Tolnay. *A Festival of Violence: An Analysis of Southern Lynchings 1882-1930*. Urbana-Chicago: University of Illinois Press, 1995.
[9] ASDMAE, Serie Politica "P" (1891-1916), b. 683, f. 882. From Italian Embassy in Washington to MAE, June 30, 1905.
[10] Cutler, 165.

Giulio Prinetti in 1902, he commented: "It is commonly assumed that lynching is a crime typical of southern states, where they are more frequent. However, the reason is probably due to the fact that in the South there are many more black people — the usual victims of mobs — than in the North."[11]

It remains that in the South, where racist ideology had deep roots, in the period of fifty years (1880-1930) during which lynching was more prevalent, one of the most reliable estimates calculates a total of 3,220 lynchings of black people and 723 whites. This is an astonishing statistic, particularly when compared to the number of episodes in the northeast (two whites and seven blacks) and in the other states with a predominantly white population, the midwest (181 whites and 79 blacks) and the Far West (447 whites and 38 blacks).[12]

Before the decade of 1880, especially in the Midwest and the West, lynching targeted primarily white people. Also targeted were Native Americans, Mexicans, Asians and African Americans. Beginning in the 1890s, when lynching became a common practice in the South, the persecutions were directed mostly at black people. Out of an average of 139 people lynched a year, 75% of them were black. The states with the highest number of lynchings were Mississippi and Louisiana, where, most of the victims were black, while in Texas the victims were mostly Mexicans.[13] On the basis of international treaties, the federal government was forced to pay reparation to the countries of origin of foreign citizen victims of these crimes. This was made necessary due to the corrupt justice system at the local level that never once was able (or willing) to identify the authors of lynchings of foreign nationals. China was the country with the highest number of victims and, consequently, received

---

[11] ASDMAE, Serie Politica, "P" (1891-1916), b. 683. From the Italian Embassy in Washington, August 4, 1902.
[12] See Brundage, p. 8. Different sources report slightly divergent statistics. The data published by Brundage are reliable.
[13] Cutler, 179.

the highest amount of compensation. Italy was second, before Mexico and Great Britain.[14]

4. Interpreting the Phenomenon

In order to understand the conditions that led to the episodes of lynching it is necessary to go beyond superficial and obvious considerations. First of all, there is no single cause that alone can explain this phenomenon.[15] The most common reductive explanation considers lynching as a residue of the past, in particular the Civil War and the ensuing Reconstruction era. Not incidentally they were more frequent in the South. However, this does not explain why lynching increased in the first years of the twentieth century and why it spread to some of the northern states where the practice, until that time, had been almost non-existent.[16]

An alarmed report was sent from the Italian embassy in Washington to Minister Enrico Morin about the spreading of this phenomenon, two years before two Italians were lynched in Erwin, Mississippi, in 1901: "In the last two months the press published daily reports of one or more episodes of lynching in the United States. Stunningly, every single previous statistic about the use of Lynch's Law has been surpassed. Not only that, but it seems that the phenomenon is no longer limited to the South, as it has spread also to northern states." Even more worrisome to the ambassador who wrote the report was the increased intensity of cruelty inflicted on the victims: "Previous crude forms of crowd justice, meant to replace legal action, seem almost benign in comparison to the horrific violence of these acts of vengeance. It's a shameful plague that defaces and offends the most elementary concepts of social and civil existence and yet it has been spreading with ghastly progression. Manhunts and summary justice followed by bloody explosions of brutal wickedness are now to be found in states like Washington, Georgia, Illinois, Massa-

---

[14] Cutler, 258-9.
[15] See Lorini, 126-8, for a review of the main interpretation of this phenomenon.
[16] See Murphey; Brundage.

chusetts, Delaware, Indiana, Alabama and Virginia. The phenomenon is now beginning to worry even Americans who still do not seem to be fully conscious of the shamefulness of such barbaric acts."[17]

Also unsatisfactory is the purely "economy-based" explanation of lynching that posits a cause-and-effect relation between the economic crisis of the 1890s and the worsening of tensions in the labor market, with a consequent surge of ethnic hatred toward foreigners. This period marks an exceptionally high increase in the migration of Italians to the United States. They represented the most recent wave of immigration and, as such, paid the highest price. This, in theory, would also explain why lynchings of Italians were prevalent in these two decades. It is necessary, however, to place each episode within a larger framework that takes into consideration the specific context in which each individual crime was perpetrated. In particular, one must observe the specific economic situation of the agricultural South, as opposed to the conditions in the West where a mining-based economy was dominant. Only with these premises and with an examination of the complex interaction of ethnic conflicts and labor-economic conflicts can one begin to ascertain the specific conditions that led to those tragic events.

Although the end of the Civil War in 1865 marked the official end of slavery, in reality the white establishment rejected the emancipation of African American former slaves. In the context of the new political and legal order, the protection of the established social and economic hierarchy, with whites at the top and blacks at the bottom, required a new, more direct justice system. From this perspective, "people's justice" was deemed necessary to complement and often replace the formal institutional tools of crime prevention and prosecution. It was a form of "justice" generally considered to be deplorable but necessary as a defensive weapon. As such it was deceptively camouflaged under the guise of a code of honor required to preserve the values, morals and rules of traditional society.

---

[17] ASDMAE, Serie Politica "P" (1891-1916), b. 683. From Italian Embassy in Washington to MAE, August 12, 1903.

The public opinion in the southern states did not consider lynching a crime. The various components of society, however, were not unanimous in the arguments used to defend it. Each group justified it in different ways, reflecting the perspectives of different social strata, economic interests and educational levels. The Italian chargé d'affaires at the Italian embassy in Washington, Marquis Guglielmo Imperiali, who had temporarily taken over from Ambassador Saverio Fava, was recalled to Italy by Minister Antonio di Rudinì after the lynching of eleven Italians in New Orleans in 1891. In his well written and well thought-out analysis, he identified three separate categories of American public opinion: "One: Some approved without reservations the mob's barbaric conduct against the Italian prisoners as a wonderful demonstration of the rights of people's sovereignty (...) Two: Some disapproved these acts in the name of civilization. These are a tiny minority yet a very important one since they come mostly from the most influential class. Three: The largest majority deplore Lynch's Law in general, however, they almost tolerate it as a national institution and they don't understand why it should not be applied to foreign citizens."[18]

A decade later, Ambassador Mayor de Planches, after new outbreaks of similar episodes in various areas, and in particular after the massacre of two Italians in Erwin, Mississippi, in 1901, sent a report with a very compelling analysis of the popular consensus surrounding lynching as a form of people's justice. He explained that it could be found across social classes while it encountered only "sterile and isolated opposition by few." He elaborated the arguments used to justify lynching at various levels of the social ladder: "The *mob* [sic] that perpetrates the lynching is composed for the most part of honest citizens who are generally crude and ignorant, live in culturally primitive conditions and dismiss or do not understand that justice can only be guaranteed when legal formalities are followed. At the same time, it is common to run into educated and civilized individuals, members of the better classes, who tend to minimize and even — in private confidential discussions — go as far as

---

[18] ASDMAE, idem, b. 445. From Italian Embassy in Washington to MAE, June 15, 1891.

justify this kind of crime, using as arguments the places where they occur, or the circumstances surrounding them, or, finally, the quality of the individuals who become its victims."[19]

The most common argument used to justify lynching was the almost total certainty that the victim was guilty, a certainty which in reality was often faulty. "Even respectable people usually comment — as an excuse for lynching — that they are never, or at least very rarely, applied to innocent and harmless people; and that in almost all cases the victims are convicted felons; and that the mob does not go after a man after he committed — or is suspected of having committed — a crime for the first time. The targets are individuals whose conduct in past has already aroused popular revulsion and who constitute real dangers to the community. Or, the community may fear that, due to some legal technicalities, they may be able to escape the punishment of justice, while the public consensus is that they are guilty or at least liable of committing other crimes."

The arguments provide self-exculpation and rest on the distrust for the effectiveness of public institutions in dealing with individuals who are, potentially or factually, guilty of a crime or previously unpunished misdeeds. Mob action is directed against individuals whom "for reasons of public safety, it is advisable to get rid of, especially in regions where, due to the vastness of the land or lack of sufficient protection by legal authorities, it is impellent on the individuals to defend themselves, their families and their properties."[20]

Not coincidentally, lynchers usually could count on the silent approval and at times the open complicity of public authorities. Judges, sheriffs, local police and prison guards therefore transformed an illegal practice into an activity that was implicitly legitimized by the institutions. Moreover, community leaders and most respected members took part more or less directly in the organization and execution of the lynchings.

---

[19] ASDMAE, idem, b. 882. From Italian Embassy in Washington to MAE, August 4, 1902.
[20] Ibidem.

Public sentiment, as represented by the press that gave it voice, was not unanimous about an issue that openly questioned citizens' fundamental right to a just trial explicitly stated in the U.S. Constitution. Many considered lynching an unacceptable and barbaric practice. However, in the southern states public opinion and the press for the most part regarded lynching, as if not exactly a good deed, at least a necessary deterrent to maintain public order and protect social hierarchy. In the South most of the press reported lynchings with an abundance of gory details about the mutilations and torture inflicted on the victims, bordering on voyeuristic morbid depravity. In many cases the press did not condemn these crimes and in quite a few cases it openly approved them. In the lynching of two Italians in Tampa, Florida, in 1910, the *Tampa Daily Times* commented that this was "a lynching and a lesson," and congratulated the mob for the impeccable organization of the operation: "The mob did a good job."[21] The operation was completed with the sale of photographs of the massacre: one of the two victims had a pipe stuck in his mouth so as to emphasize his "Italian-ness." This ghoulish iconographic merchandising was finally stopped after the protest by the Italian consul.[22]

5. ITALIANS AS SEEN BY AMERICANS

My work reconstructing the episodes of lynching of Italians and the protests presented to the United States government by the Italian government does not dwell on the question of whether the victims were innocent or guilty of the crimes they were accused of. The first reason is that most cases had not been adjudicated by the legal system, thus the issue of "legal" status of their alleged culpability is moot. The second reason is that, whether innocent or guilty, all the victims had the absolute right to a fair and impartial trial. I did not want to give in to easy

---

[21] Asdmae, Serie Z, Usa, b.33, f.27/2. From Italian Consulate in New Orleans to Mae, October 8, 1910.
[22] "Governor Stops Sale of Lynching Pictures." In *The Tampa Daily Times*, September 27, 1910.

generalizations and stereotypes of any kind, neither with the exaltation of "hard-working Italians, tenacious in hardships and frugal,"[23] nor with scorn for the "ugly, dirty and mean" criminals, quick with a knife, mafiosi and troublemakers.

American public opinion, in particular in southern states such as Louisiana, where xenophobia was more explicit, was not particularly kind toward Italian immigrants who were preceded by a reputation of being subversive "hot-heads." Although the lynching of Italians was almost never politically motivated, they paid the price for being the latest in a series of waves of immigrants to arrive in the United States. Compared to the workers of the old emigration waves, they were seen as low-cost labor and potential replacements in the case of labor strikes.[24] The real fear of competition for low-paying jobs fed a climate of anti-Italian discrimination with deep roots in the economic situation.

Americans reacted with suspicion to the complex issue of the role of Italian immigrants. These, in turn, found themselves embroidered in the chaotic "clash encounters" of many different cultures in the period straddling the nineteenth and the twentieth centuries. The consular officer for immigration in New Orleans, Count Gerolamo Moroni, charged by the Italian authorities with the task of investigating cases of lynching of Italians, in a report in 1908 observed the conditions of the labor market. Italians were caught in a harsh environment of fierce competition with salaried workers from other ethnic groups. In addition, they had to face very difficult circumstances in their relations with their employers who regarded them as "beasts of burden."

Moroni wrote: "In my opinion Italians are sought after but are not appreciated. They are sought after by employers because they are more productive and work non-stop, but employers love them the way they could love a beast of burden." Moroni also found that the relations of Italians and "lower class Americans" was rife with acrid conflicts, because Americans "see in them dangerous competitors that caused salaries to

---

[23] The definition is found in A. Pierantoni, "Il linciaggio negli Stati Uniti e la emigrazione italiana." In *Italia Coloniale*. 1904, 6, p. 51.
[24] In the original *crumiri*, equivalent to *scabs*. [FGC]

drop." Even small Italian businesses were hostile toward them because of their obsession with saving. "Unlike Americans and blacks who spend every penny they earn in their stores, our people save with the goal of starting their own businesses or to send money back to Italy."[25] Also very common was the other stereotype, the folkloric portrayal of Italian immigrants best defined as mafiosi and tagged with the nickname *dagos*, with a knife in their pockets (unlike Americans who carried handguns). The report drafted by the grand jury investigating the 1891 New Orleans lynching reads: "Their deadly weapon of choice is the easier-to-conceal knife or stiletto, used to stab the victim in the chest or in the back [...] Their all-consuming motive is vendetta."[26]

Just because Italians were dark-skinned they were not automatically associated with white people. They were actually regarded as "intermediate" between blacks and whites, in particular in the South where the hierarchical order based on skin color was much more rigid. In the case of five Italians lynched in Tallulah, in Madison Parish, Louisiana, in 1899, the magazine *Harper's Weekly* wrote that the execution grew out of a climate of racial clashes between the white minority in power and the overwhelming majority of poor, powerless black people, the usual victims of lynching. The wave of Italian immigrants added a third, unwelcome, guest to the party. Italians were not black but, just the same, they were not accepted by the white minority as part of their own group. Thus, at the first opportunity, whites used lynching to send a clear message to Italians about their standing and position on the social and ethnic pyramid: "White people who govern and administer Madison are not willing to admit Italians to their ranks."[27]

The racial identity of Italians was not tied to the color of their skin but the majority opinion among Americans was that Italians were not white. In the words of a Seattle, Washington, journalist commenting on

---

[25] G. Moroni. "L'emigrazione italiana nel distretto consolare di Nuova Orleans". In *Bollettino dell'Emigrazione,* 1908, 16, p. 25.
[26] *Report of the Grand Jury,* May 5, 1891, in FRUS 1891, p. 719.
[27] N. Walzer. "Tallulah's Shame" in *Harper's Weekly,* August 5, 1899.

an alleged lynching[28] in 1892 that never took place: "Italians and Chinese are not considered part of the white race." One of the speakers at the Second Convention of Italians Abroad, held in Rome in 1911, Luigi Scala claimed that in the South there seemed to exist a sort of equivalence between Italians and blacks. He attributed it to the friendliness that Italians showed toward blacks, because, as he stated: "They don't feel toward them the kind of innate repugnance that Americans from the southern states feel (…) Indeed, sometimes they live with black women as husband-and-wife and sometimes even openly."[29] The familiarity between Italians and blacks, however, was limited to a few states in the South, among them Louisiana. As always happens to people who are kept on the lowest rungs of the social ladder, the rest of Italians, even when they were victims of discrimination, were rather willing to discriminate against others, in an attempt to differentiate themselves from those who were regarded as inferior, namely the Chinese and the "lazy and ever-complaining blacks,"[30] as the Italian press at that time often portrayed them.

The Italian diplomatic and consular personnel dealing with immigrants did not always treat them with dignity and respect. Their role as "public defenders," that is, the tasks of protecting and defending, was discharged effectively only in certain cases, while in the majority of circumstances it was lacking and perfunctory. The confidential reports filed with the Ministry of Foreign Affairs reveal an aristocratically detached attitude. Despite the fact that they were the only official entities in the position to help, defend and protect the immigrants, rarely did consulates and embassy get involved in the myriad of daily problems brought to them by a mass of mostly poor and illiterate southern Italians. Facing the "indefensible" Italian colony in New Orleans, notorious for its inter-

---

[28] "A Murder Avenged. Four Italians Assassins Hanged in the Woods" in *The Seattle Press-Time"* June 17, 1892.
[29] L. Scala. "Poche considerazioni giuridiche e sociali su l'emigrazione italiana negli Stati Uniti e particolarmente in Louisiana" in *Congresso degli Italiani all'estero*. Roma 1913, p. 19.
[30] *La Tribuna*. August 24, 1901.

nal feuds, for crime and the mafia, the Italian minister in a letter to the local consul in 1910 recommended that the Italian consular authorities not get involved to the extent possible: "I don't believe it is the case to show an interest for such malefactors."[31] The overwhelming majority of Italian immigrants was in a state of poverty and needed the support, economic and otherwise, of the their consulates. Legal expenses, for instance, were outrageously high. Attorney Gino Speranza, secretary of the society for the protection of Italian immigrants in New York, in 1903 calculated that to initiate legal action that included lawyers and a search for witnesses a minimum of $10,000 — an exorbitant figure in those days — was needed.[32] Also, the Catholic Church was rather silent when faced with cases of lynching of Italians, thus compounding the standoffish attitude of the consular authorities. This was due in part to its limited presence in the states in which the episodes took place (Louisiana, Mississippi, Colorado, Florida), where Protestant denominations were dominant. Another reason may be the fact that an Apostolic Delegation was installed in Washington only in 1892.[33]

6. Italy vs. the United States

The reoccurrence of these violent episodes and, most of all, their frequency made official relations between Italy and the United States rather difficult and, for over two decades, caused extremely bitter diplomatic controversies. The 1891 New Orleans lynching in particular —

---

[31] ASDMAE, Consulate of New Orleans, b. 1, 1st versamento. From MAE to Consulate of Italy in New Orleans, August 1, 1910.

[32] ASDMAE. Serie Politica "P" (1891-1916), b, 680, f. 856. From Italian Embassy in Washington to MAE, May 20, 1903.

[33] M. Sanfilippo. "Fonti ecclesiastiche per la storia dell'emigrazione e dei gruppi etnici nel Nord America: gli Stati Uniti" in *Studi Emigrazione*, December 1955, 120, p. 623. After the lynching of eleven Italians in New Orleans in 1891, the Scalabrinian Father Giacomo Gambera who had been living there since 1889, turned to Mother Cabrini, asking that a group of missionaries from her congregation be sent to open a school for the children of that wounded and demoralized community. The missionaries arrived in 1892. See G. Rosoli. "Archivio dei missionary di S. Carlo (Scalabriniani)" in *Studi Emigrazione*, December 1896, 124, p. 696.

although it wasn't the first lynching of Italians to take place — marked the beginning of a protracted contention between the two governments. Previously, there had been several clear signals that an atmosphere of anti-Italian discrimination was intensifying in several states. Against this backdrop the New Orleans episode made the mood even more volatile and exasperated, resulting in other cases with the same sort of rituals. The climate in which the massacre came to fruition was preceded by smaller but not less-alarming episodes that were reported by the Italian press published in the United States.

This episode triggered a very strong reaction even at the international level. Eleven Italians, some of whom were awaiting trial while others had been already acquitted, were forcibly removed from jail by a mob and lynched in public with the in-your-face acquiescence of the authorities. The importance of this event goes beyond the fact itself, grave as it was, in that it marks the beginning of a serious and complicated crisis in the history of Italian–American relations and led to the recall by Italy of its ambassador to the United States — the first and only time this has ever happened — followed by a similar measure by the American government. When the acrimony between the two countries reached its peak, the American press went as far as ventilating the possibility that Italy might declare war. Most of all, it was the first time that a foreign government forced the Congress of the United States to face the request of a constitutional amendment to correct the unbalance between the powers of federal government and the rights of individual states in matters concerning the crime of lynching of foreign citizens and their protection, or lack thereof.

The origin of the legal contention was the American government's failure to honor the treaty signed by the United States and Italy on February 26, 1871.[34] The reciprocally binding agreement stipulated that foreign citizens of the two countries would enjoy the protection of the local authorities and, consequently, would be treated as equal. Based on

---

[34] The text of the treaty can be found in MAE *Trattati e Convenzioni fra il Regno d'Italia e i governi esteri.* Vol. IV (contains treaties and conventions signed between January 1, 1870 and January 1, 1873.) Rome, 1874, pp.144-55.

the same treaty, the opposite was also true: foreign citizens were not entitled to privileges or favorable treatment. With the New Orleans lynching of 1891 a gigantic problem surfaced in the American legislation, a problem that became explosive. The U.S. Constitution grants the individual states considerable autonomy, particularly with regard to the legal system; an autonomy that the federal government cannot curtail. This issue rose to the level of institutional conflict concerning the rights — considered as sacred and non-negotiable — of individual states to manage autonomously their judicial powers. At the same time, the federal government was under the obligation to fulfill the international treaty that granted agreed-upon reciprocal protection to the citizens of the two nations.

This anomaly in the U.S. Constitution for Italians resident in America was the source of considerable worries, given the difficulty in finding a "technical" solution that could be also politically palatable. The paradox consisted in the fact that the president of the United States represented the whole country in the context of the relations with foreign powers, but at the same time he had no jurisdiction on the individual states that constitute the federation. In other words, he represented the whole but not the parts that form the whole. Consequently, the president of the United States had the right to hold foreign governments accountable for offenses against American citizens on their territories while he was unable to honor his obligations since the Constitution did not allow him to interfere in the autonomy of individual states. The fundamental clause of reciprocity was *de facto* void.

The problem therefore became both formal and political. The formal aspect consisted in the fact that a government's interference in the internal legislation of a state would be a violation of the Constitution and, consequently, the government was prevented from implementing international treaties stipulated with foreign nations. The political problem was perhaps considered even more important by the federal government. It consisted in the risk, if not the outright certainty, of a defeat in a presidential election for any candidate, presidents included, who had included in his program a law that would curtail state rights, and most of all a specific federal law against lynching. The result would have been the guaranteed loss of the states whose autonomy was challenged, first of all the southern states. Such an initiative would have also meant the risk of a political crisis with a deep split between North and South only a few years after the end of the Civil War when the old wounds were still open.

7. The Problem of Citizenship

The issue of citizenship had an enormous importance in the relations between Italy and the United States. Contrary to the provisions of international treaties that guaranteed reciprocal protection to the respective citizens, non-American citizens — i.e., aliens — in the United States received different treatment. In the diplomatic arm-wrestling matches caused by the lynching of Italians, the American government tried more than once to pass as Americans even individuals who had just started the process of naturalization. Based on a rather elastic interpretation of their status those individuals, according to American government, were no longer entitled to the protection of the Italian embassy.

The naturalization process at that time had several steps and only when it was fully completed could a foreigner be considered a citizen of the United States. However, in some states, thanks to their sovereign rights, individuals were considered citizens with the right to vote even before the five-year residence requirement of the federal process had been completed.

A rigid and uniform norm on naturalization was imposed on the states only after the lynching of five Italians in Tallulah. The language used to pay reparation to the families of the Italian victims was a masterpiece of diplomatic acrobatics: on the one hand it acknowledged that the victims had been done wrong, but at the same time it rejected the request for payment of a indemnification. The moneys were disbursed to the families under the guise of an act of mercy, without the acknowledgement of any responsibility in the matter. The language used to justify the indemnification stated that the payment was "as a concession without reference to the question of responsibility of the United States."

This formula contained a blatant contradiction since on the one hand it indemnified *de facto* the families of the victims, but on the other it implicitly affirmed that the federal government did not have the authority to intervene in crimes that were under the jurisdiction of individual states.

In the cases of lynching of Italians, to avoid international complications, in practically every case the American government tried to demonstrate that the victims had already obtained American citizenship. If successful, this would deprive the Italian government of the right and duty to intervene to protect what would amount to a former citizen. Until 1899 the problem, however, was quite complex. The naturalization process began at first with the application for citizenship of the state of residence and ended with the granting of American citizenship by the federal government. In the case of lynching of Italians until 1899, the federal government adopted a flexible interpretation of the norms. It considered as American citizens individuals who had obtained state citizenship and had applied for "federal naturalization" even if the requirement of five years of residence had not been met.

Italy's Ambassador Fava regarded the American interpretation as purely instrumental and defended, with reason, "the principle that the naturalization to the United States can only be granted by federal laws and not those of the states." Furthermore, he stressed that "the universally accepted doctrine [is] that the simple expression of an intention does not grant citizenship." Only in 1899, after the lynching in Tallulah, did the federal government establish once and for all the criterion that foreigners could not become citizens of the United States until they formally received the legal papers granting citizenship.

From the Italian side, the legislation was always very strict when it came to allowing citizens to "lose" their citizenship. According to the Crispi Law of 1888 and the following Giolitti Law of 1901, the offspring of Italian citizens were themselves Italian citizens, with no exceptions — for males — for what pertained to the obligatory military service and call to arms in war time. Fulfillment of military obligations was mandatory for all emigrants and even for children of emigrants who had not renounced Italian citizenship.[35] For the Italian state the principle of *jus sanguinis* (the "right of blood") prevailed over the *jus loci* (the "right of soil") valid in the United States, on the basis of which it was sufficient to be born on American soil to be automatically entitled to U.S. citizenship.

The formal issue concerning American citizenship was thus solved in 1899. However, the issue of the constitutional anomaly regarding the relations between federal government and individual states still remained an open question. The fact that the issue had been raised by a foreign country, in this case Italy, added even more complications. Any constitutional change resulting from pressure from the outside by a foreign country that "dared" criticize the constitutional framework by highlighting its incoherence with respect to the obligations subscribed in international treaties would have given the appearance of "weakness" by the American government. After eleven Italians were lynched in New Orleans, in the thick of a diplomatic crisis, American Ambassador to Italy Albert Porter, in a private conversation with Minister Antonio di Rudinì, expressed the disappointment of American citizens for the conduct of the Italian government. Porter stated that "American public opinion was irritated at the threatening tone of the Italian government that gave the impression of undue pressure on the American government without giving it time to discuss the issue."[36]

In addition to a general resistance to make changes to the Constitution, spurious reasons were also raised on "quantitative" considerations, such as the fact that the number of Europeans who had been lynched was not high enough to justify revising the foundations of the constitutional chart.

---

[35] Crispi legislation, n. 5866, November 30, 1888. Giolitti legislation, n. 25, January 31, 1901.
[36] ASDMAE, Serie Politica "P" (1891-1916), b, 445. From MAE to Italian Embassu in Washington, May 28, 1891.

This was the argument put forth by Undersecretary for Foreign Affairs Alfredo Baccelli in his answer in the Lower House of Parliament (*Camera dei Deputati*) to a question by Representative Benedetto Cirmeni, who opposed the Italian government's acceptance of an indemnification for the families of Italians lynched in Erwin in 1901. Baccelli remarked that: "in comparison to a few lynchings of Europeans per year, there are at least 150 lynchings a year of American citizens. It is very difficult in these circumstances to apply direct pressure aimed at changing American legislation."[37]

The issue represented a source of embarrassment for the American government, particularly after the New Orleans massacre that triggered a strong formal protest by the Italian government — albeit without causing a full-blown diplomatic crisis. In confidential conversations with the various Italian ambassadors, unlike in official statements, American representatives manifested a sense of unease followed by several attempts to arrive at a solution that could reconcile the technical and legal aspects with political prudence. President Grover Cleveland's position was: "Something must be done."[38] Officially, however, tones and style always reflected a tenacious arrogance and a staunch defense of American institutions, all the while formally condemning the practice of lynching.

The reparation given by the federal government to the families of Italian victims was presented as "charity" and was considered offensive by Italian communities in the United States as well as by the great majority of the Italian parliament. Italian communities, usually divided and in constant conflict with each other, for once stood firm and steadfast in their vocal denunciations of the crimes and in their demands for protection. The Italian-language press in the United States was unanimous in denouncing tenaciously the monstrosity of the crimes perpetrated by "civilized" Americans against "uncivilized" Italians. There was also a

---

[37] Minutes of Parliamentary sessions (Atti Parlamentari, AP), Camera dei Deputati, Legislatura XXI, Discussioni, Session of May 7, 1903. The discussion was reported in *The New York Times*, "Italian Views of the Lynchings in America." May 8, 1903.
[38] ADMAE, Serie Politica "P" (1891-1916), b. 605, f. 517. From the Embassy of Italy in Washington to MAE, March 14, 1895.

general attitude of distrust and disillusionment, bordering on resignation and fatalism, about the mechanisms at work in American institutions and the concrete possibility of constitutional changes. After the Erwin lynchings, an Italian newspaper commented: "For Italian immigrants the risk of falling victim of yellow fever in Brazil is equal to the risk of being lynched in the U.S.A."[39] At the same time the conduct of the embassy was disheartening. It seemed that Italian representatives considered it more important to discourage new waves of immigrants from Italy than to defend effectively Italian nationals. In a letter to Minister Tittoni, Ambassador Mayor de Planches in 1905 wrote: "The persistence of these two kinds of crime, lynching and 'peonage' [forced detention workers ...] should suggest caution and prudence in giving advice to potential immigrants."[40]

The Italian communities were so accustomed and resigned to the lack of concern — if not outright complicity — by American authorities in the case of lynchings of fellow countrymen that they actually officially thanked the governor of Colorado when he took action and offered a $1,000 reward — the only time something like this happened — for the capture of the lynching of five Italians in Walsen-burg, Colorado, in 1895. The governor's initiative was for naught. Nevertheless, the Italian community, in a state of near disbelief, donated to him a framed ornate parchment gratefully honoring him for "his concern and impartiality, despite the fact that he just did his job of trying to identify the culprits of a heinous crime — but a job that authorities at the local level hadn't even bothered to start."[41] On the other side it should be mentioned that, as Italian Acting Consul Carlo Papini rightly argued after the Tallulah lynching, authorities would expose themselves to great danger if they were to conduct an active investigation given the climate of diffuse hostility and collective refusal to cooperate with the law. This was well

---

[39] "Erwineide" in "*L'Araldo*". New York, January 25, 1901.
[40] ASDMAE, Serie Politica "P" (1891-1916), b, 683, f. 882. From the Italian Embassy in Washington to MAE, June 30, 1905.
[41] ASDMAE, Serie Politica "P" (1891-1916), b, 605, f. 517. From the Italian consulate in Denver to the Embassy of Italy in Washington, April 12, 1895.

known to the sheriff of Tallulah who at first seemed concerned with solving the crime but "after turning the other way, now doesn't want to take the chance of ending up like our fellow-countrymen by revealing the names of the perpetrators, unless he were forced to do so by a superior authority and only after receiving immunity and being relocated to a different place."[42]

8. America's Italians against Italy

The Italian-language press did not limit its vehement protest to local public authorities. Just as loud and persistent were the denunciations of insufficient and inefficient protection of Italians by the Italian government and its consular and diplomatic representatives. The indignation expressed through the press was such that some feared it would ignite a spiral of vengeance followed by reprisals against Italians. In the case of the New Orleans lynching there were explicit calls to react: "No laments, vengeance"[43] screamed an Italian newspaper. In other cases of lynching against Italians, the offense demanded reparation. To stem the tide, Italian ambassadors sent very strong directives to the consuls asking that they pacify the communities by encouraging trust in the activity of the diplomats and in the protection of the Italian government. After the lynching of an Italian in Denver, Colorado, in 1893, the consul went as far as dissuading Italians from participating in the victim's funeral, with the exception of the closest relatives.[44]

At times not even a lynching satisfied the lust for blood of insatiable mobs, and the risk of violence against Italians persisted. Only a month after the Tallulah massacre the threat of a lynching targeted the relative of one of the victims whose only "guilt" was that he moved to town from outside to take over one of the victims' business. The lynching was pre-

---

[42] ASDMAE, Serie Politica "P" (1891-1916), b. 656. From the Italian consulate in New Orleans to the Italian Embassy in Washington, July 29, 1899.

[43] "Mass-Meeting contro i vigliacchi e assassini" in *L'Eco d'Italia*. New York, March 14, 1891.

[44] ASDMAE, Serie Politica "P" (1891- 1916), b. 591. From the Italian consulate in Denver to MAE, July 31, 1893.

vented thanks to a tip from an informant who gave the unfortunate Italian enough time to flee with his family, leaving behind his store. Eventually, three years later and after a long and protracted legal battle, he was compensated by an act of Congress.

This was the real sore point: Italian immigrants looked with distrust and disenchantment at the chance of obtaining justice from the American government, and similar distrust and disenchantment were fed by the inability of the Italian government to stand up to their American counterparts. "It is useless to spend money for ambassadors and embassies"[45] was the thunderous headline of a report from the United States published by the Italian newspaper *La Tribuna*, indignant at the usual ineffectiveness of the Italian government after the killing of an Italian in Ashdown, Arkansas, in 1901.

The Italian press, however, failed to mention the resistance to testify by the Italians from the communities where the lynchings took place, both when the investigation was conducted by American authorities and by Italian consuls and their agents. The reticence was caused by fear of retaliation, in a climate of heavy intimidation that, according to the various consuls, made it difficult to "nail" the culprits of the lynchings. According to Acting Consul Papini "generally, Italian witnesses are quick to make grand and magniloquent statements in front of the representatives of their native country, but when they are in front of a grand jury, either because they lack a conscience or because they are intimidated, or because of weakness or pressure, with the same ease they change their stories or completely recant previous depositions."[46] There was no effective alternative to eye-witness testimonies that could lead to the identification of the authors of lynchings. Not even local private detectives would help. After the massacre of two Italians in Erwin, the embassy forwarded to the ministry the information received by the consular agent in charge: "Private investigation agencies as well as detectives from the secret police declined to pursue the case. This fits with the customs of

---

[45] *La Tribuna*, August 24, 1901.
[46] ASDMAE, Serie Politica "P" (1891-1916). From the Italian consulate in New Orleans to MAE, October 15, 1901.

the South, where lynching is not considered a crime, and also where anybody who tried to track down the assassins would seriously imperil himself."[47]

9. INDEMNIFICATION: "THE BLOOD PRICE"

The tone of the Italian-language press in the United States became even harsher after the Erwin lynching and after the usual humiliation of an indemnification granted as "charity" as compensation for the lack of an investigation and punishment of the killers by the state and federal governments. In this case of justice-not-done, the New York-based Italian newspaper *L'Araldo* screamed its outrage against the acceptance of indemnification by Italian Minister of Foreign Affairs Prinetti, accusing him of a "state crime" and attacking him with never-heard-before words. "The Italian Parliament should have done its duty of expelling that minister from the House," the very same minister who in parliament had the gall to declare that from that moment onward he would defend the Italians in the United States but "not with excessive vigor."[48]

The monetary value of the indemnification granted by the American government, described by Italian-language press as "blood price," was also considered inadequate. Again, *L'Araldo* criticized the miserly amount given as reparation for the Erwin lynching, totaling $5,000 for the victims' families. In comparison "American tribunals award reparations amounting to 30 or 50 or a 100,000 dollars to the unfortunate victims of train accidents or explosions which are unplanned events and not premeditated the way lynchings are."[49]

The heavy climate of resentment was not tempered by the sarcasm of a part of the American press that added its own commentary to the

---

[47] ASDMAE, Italian Diplomatic Delegation in Washington (1901-1909), b. 147, f. 3225. From the Italian Embassy in Washington to MAE, August 14, 1901.
[48] "Erwineide" in *L'Araldo*, New York, May 9, 1903. In reality, Minister Prinetti used different words, declaring that in favor of Italians abroad he would apply a "non-swashbuckling protection." AP, Senato del Regno, Legislatura XXI, Discussioni, Session of December 20, 1901.
[49] "Erwineide," ibidem May.

meagerness of the indemnification. In a parliamentary question in the Italian Lower House, Representative Cirmeni warned about the risk that the government was taking in accepting the compensation to the families of the victims of the Erwin lynching. He referred to a cartoon published in an Italian-language newspaper in the United States showing the American secretary of state in the act of handing over a purse to the Italian ambassador with the following caption: "These Italians are so cheap that it may be worth it to lynch them all."[50] The bitter irony of the cartoon had made an impression and had circulated widely attracting lots of comments in the Italian media and in the parliament, reinforcing the position of those in the Senate, among whom was former Ambassador Fava, who already in 1901 were in favor of a dignified rejection of the indemnification.[51]

The Italian press also raised the alarm about possible future violence against Italians in the United States, given the streak of lynchings, the connivance of American authorities, the inevitable impunity of the killers, and finally the humiliating blood price. In the Italian parliament, particularly after the Erwin lynching, there was a very emotional debate with parliamentary questions and accusations against the government for its lukewarm response and its routine of perfunctory protests against the crimes followed by a very accommodating willingness to close the case after the blood price was paid. Initially, after each episode of lynching, the Italian embassy issued firm protests to the federal government, with strong words condemning the impunity of the killers that the Minister of Foreign Affairs Prinetti described as "open encouragement to future killings of which, tragically, our fellow countrymen are repeatedly the victims."[52] After the Erwin lynching, Ambassador Francesco Carignani recommended to the minister that the formal protest be followed by the

---

[50] AP, Camera dei Deputati, Legislatura XXI, Discussioni, Session of May 7, 1903. The Parliamentary question with the comment to the comic was also reported by *The New York Times,* "Views of the Lynchings in America." May 8, 1903, 5.

[51] AP, Senato del Regno, Legislatura XXI, Discussioni, Session of December 20, 1901.

[52] ASDMAE, Rappresentanza Diplomatica Italiana in Washington (1901-1909), b. 147, f. 3225. From MAE to Italian Embassy in Washington, October 10, 1901.

threat to denounce the Treaty of February 26, 1871.[53] The recommendation was not implemented. As usual, after the initial indignation and protest, and after taking into account the power relations between the two countries and their respective weights on the international scene, the tendency to take a "realistic" position always prevailed in the Italian government. The government also gave careful consideration to the need of the North American outlet for a growing number of Italians who, temporarily or permanently, were forced to leave the country.

The "realism" of the Italian government in accepting the blood price was very unpopular in the Italian communities in the United States as well as in the parliament. After the Erwin massacre, Senator Fava strongly attacked Minister Prinetti in the Senate. He accused him of not reacting forcefully enough to the grand jury's verdict that attributed the lynching to "an act of God."[54] Fava maintained that if the government had rejected the indemnification, the dignity and prestige of the country would have benefited, particularly if the refusal had been followed by strong pressure for reforms of the U.S. Constitution.

His proposal was not followed up. The Italian government did not take either the initiative of rejecting or accepting the indemnification offered by the federal government to the victims' families. It simply chose not to oppose it. The indemnification, however, did not soothe the wounds either in Italy or in the Italian colonies in America. Nevertheless, the attitude of the Italian government did not change. After the lynching of two Italians in Tampa, Florida, in 1910, confronted with the customary offer of indemnification by the federal government, Italian Ambassador Luigi Cusani didn't manifest any outrage at the monstrosity of a jury verdict that had failed to punish the lynching's organizers — the latest in a series of humiliations inflicted on the Italian government. Indeed, he considered it a great victory the fact that Congress, after a three-year delay, allocated the amount of $6,000, three times the

---

[53] ASDMAE, ibidem. From Italian Embassy in Washington to MAE, October 10, 1901.
[54] AP, Senato del Regno, Legislatura XXI, Discussioni, Tornata of December 20, 1901.

standard amount paid to victims' families after the lynching of a foreign citizen (only one of the two Italians was still a citizen of Italy).[55] After this "success," the ambassador instructed the consulates to publicize with great emphasis this rich result in the various Italian communities, so that they would come to appreciate the effects of their government's protection.[56]

10. Changing the American Constitution?

In the period when lynchings of Italians took place, each conflict between the two countries on this issue led systematically to the same conclusion; namely, impunity for the killers and an indemnification as an act of charity. The American government, however, wasn't always totally inflexible. After the assassination of President William McKinley, who had seemed more responsive to the Italian protests, the new President Theodore Roosevelt, elected in 1901, chose a more defensive and conservative approach. This resulted in a reduced sensitivity toward the lynching problem and less concern for the image of the United States on the international stage.

In reality, the United States, thanks to its powerful position in the world, never showed particular embarrassment in front of the criticism of European governments concerning the practice of lynching. Despite the fact that the New Orleans episode had caused general condemnation at the international level, Italian chargé d'affaires Imperiali suggested that the traditional arrogance of American nationalism would not be even minimally undermined. In a report to the minister, he wrote: "The condemnation of the United States by civilized Europe didn't produce any effect whatsoever, be it because for the American masses the rest of

---

[55] VEDI SITO
[56] ASDMAE, Serie "Z", Usa, b. 33, f. 27/2. From Italian Embassy in Washington to all Consulates of Italy in the United States, November 20, 1913.

the world does not exist, be it because the press failed to report what was being said against this government on the other side of the Atlantic."[57]

In the press only a few voices expressing a different sensibility on this issue could be heard. The *New York Tribune*, for instance, after the Erwin incident, sided with the protests of the "patient" Italian government and the demand that international treaties be observed, arguing that the U.S. government's conduct may become the Turkish government, but not the American. "The Italian government showed a lot of patience but there is a limit to the gracious toleration for a situation that we would expect from Turkey, with its genius for diplomatic irresponsibility, and not from the United States."[58]

From the first episodes of lynching of Italians until the Tallulah case in 1899, the federal government, prevented by the Constitution from taking any measures, appealed to the various state governors pressing them to abide by the provisions of international treaties in hopes that this would be enough to find and try the offenders. Only after Tallulah did the government, for the first time, send a federal agent from the Justice Department to conduct a special investigation on the slaughter. This case, thus, thanks primarily to the hard, relentless and intricate diplomatic work of Ambassador Fava, represented a major development, in that for the first time there was the implicit recognition of the principle that the federal government had the right to interfere in the internal affairs of a state.

The investigation, however, ran into the unanimous refusal by local police forces and by the population to cooperate. In this regard, the answer given in private by Secretary of State John Hay to Ambassador Fava is illuminating. Fava wrote that, in explaining the reason why the American official refused to disclose the results of the investigation: "He re-

---

[57] ASDMAE, Serie Politica "P" (1891-1916), b, 445. From Italian Embassy in Washington to MAE, June 15, 1891.
[58] *New York Tribune*, December 27, 1901.

peated that he would not reveal the content because he was ashamed of his country."⁵⁹

At the same time, Ambassador Fava claimed the breakthrough as a personal victory and went on to overestimate the chance of future developments. In his view the sophisticated diplomatic work of the Italian embassy in the Tallulah case had, contrary to what had happened in previous episodes, succeeded in injecting into public opinion and that of, the president and Congress, the concept that a constitutional change was necessary and urgent. Previously, in 1892, an attempt to modify the Constitution had been tried and failed when a bill introduced by Senator Joseph Dolph was harshly attacked in the Senate for being unconstitutional. Something, however, seemed to be moving after Tallulah. At the opening of Congress in December 1899 and in the following year President McKinley, due to the constant pressure of Ambassador Fava on Secretary of State Hay, in a message to Congress suggested that two bills, respectively by Senator Cushman Davis and Congressman Robert Hitt, should be promptly approved. The goal was to transfer to the federal courts the entire jurisdiction of international cases.⁶⁰ Most of all, for the first time ever a president of the United States felt the need to fill a constitutional hole. "It is our duty to fill the constitutional vacuum that brought us, and could bring us again, to such deadly results."⁶¹ The Senate committee approved the bill with unanimous vote, but not with enough time to bring it to the floor before the end of the legislature. The genius of the bill was that it did not appear to have punitive intentions toward the autonomy of individual states. In fact it stipulated that crimes committed against foreigners would be adjudicated in federal court but under the laws of the state where the crime took place. This

---

⁵⁹ ASDMAE, Serie Politica "P" (1891-1916), b. 656. ASDMAE From Italian Embassy in Washington to MAE, April 24, 1900.
⁶⁰ F.S. Fava. "I linciaggi agli Stati Uniti. La questione giuridica". In *Nuova Antologia*, 1902, p. 645.
⁶¹ ASDMAE, Serie Politica "P" (1891-1916), b. 656. From Italian Embassy in Washington to MAE, December 3, 1900.

concession aimed at protecting the jurisdictional prerogatives of every state.

After the assassination of McKinley in 1901, Theodore Roosevelt, his successor, did not show particular attention to this issue. In his message to the new Congress in December 1901 he did not even mention the problem. His firm and steady condemnation of lynching did not translate into congressional initiatives, nor in resuming the previous year's debate. On the occasion of Memorial Day on May 31, 1902, in his speech, President Roosevelt execrated lynchings as "barbaric and cruel" acts and "a shame for our people," without making reference to the protection due to foreigners against this practice. The anti-lynching legislation that had died at the end of the previous Congress would never be introduced again. Behind its failure was the strong opposition by many members, which reflected a similarly strong resistance by the states that did not accept even a small reduction of their autonomy. In those years, however, the internal debate in the United States about the increase in lynchings became more animated, thanks in part to the relentless activity of Ambassador Fava. Senator Jacob Gallinger from New Hampshire, in the 57th Congress in 1902 introduced a resolution to charge the Senate Judiciary Committee with the task of conducting an investigation on lynchings, with the mandate to refer back to the Senate about possible solutions that would conform to the current laws and the Constitution. Once again the issue of federal power and state rights was surfacing, although it was not directly related to the lynching of foreigners and the respect of international treaties.

Beyond the legal aspects concerning jurisdiction, Senator Gallinger made public statistics that denounced an upward trend in lynchings and in the number of states where they were taking place that now included also northern states. Alarms were raised at the tortures that preceded and followed the murders and even at the fact that the victims often were accused of crimes that did not appear particularly grievous. The typical crime that allegedly unleashed the "legitimate" reaction culminating in the lynching was an act of violence against a white woman by a black rapist — although the rationale did not apply to white men guilty of raping black women. In reality, rape was not the most frequent justification for lynching. In many cases lynchings took place for senseless reasons.[62] Senator Gallinger's proposal to vote immediately on his recommendations did not obtain the unanimity required, primarily due to the opposition of the mostly racist southern states. It was therefore delayed,[63] and with the delay fell all the hopes of the Italian embassy.

At the same time the resistance against interference by the federal government in order to honor international treaties began to soften a bit, with the restriction that a possible change would only concern the protection of foreigners and not that of American citizens. It was no coincidence that after the 1910 Tampa lynching, the opposition monthly *Crisis* commented with irony on the bitter hypocrisy of indemnifying only the families of foreign citizens and not those of African Americans. The contradiction could not be more strident: the most frequent victims of lynching were denied reparation because they enjoyed the "privilege" of being American citizens.[64]

The Tampa episode marked the end of lynchings of Italians. The same cannot be said of discriminations, maltreatment and abuses that continued for decades surrounded by the indifference of the majority of Americans and the protest, mostly for naught, of Italian authorities. Still in 1920, almost thirty years after the first contention between the Italian and the American governments, Congress was busy discussing, without producing any result, whether to accept the President William Taft proposal contemplating that in case of lynching of foreign citizens, the federal government and not the states should have jurisdiction.[65] In the decade between 1930 and 1940, the number of lynchings started declin-

---

[62] Proof of this came from the courageous denunciation campaign by African American journalist Ida B. Wells toward the end of the nineteenth century. A reconstruction of her activity is in Lorini *Cartoline dall'inferno*, p.120-5.
[63] Cutler, *Lynch-Law*, p. 260.
[64] *Crisis* was the publication of the NAACP (National Association for the Advancement of Colored People) directed by W.E.B. Du Bois from 1910 to 1937.
[65] "Aliens and their Treaty Rights" in *Hearings Before the Committee on the Judiciary*, House of Representatives, Sixty-sixth Congress, Second Session, on H.R., 259, 4123 and 11873. Government Printing Office, Washington, 1920, p. 15.

ing, at first in the West and in the North-east, and later in the South. Some of the reasons were related to social, political and economic conditions, but the largest credit goes to the activism of the many associations born to fight the endemic plague of lynching in the south. The most active was the National Association for the Advancement of Colored People (NAACP.) The weak legal provisions put in place by the various states against the spread of lynchings beginning in the 1890s were never effective as a deterrent, mostly for the reason that they were only partially or not at all enforced.[66]

This explains the mobilization of activists, not just African American, pushing for the approval of federal anti-lynching legislation. Even this most determined mobilization was met with great, insurmountable resistance. During the 1930s President Franklin Delano Roosevelt himself, who had shown considerable openness on the issue of civil rights, did not lead the charge for he could not give up the electoral support of white voters in southern states. Anti-lynching legislation would have turned the electorate of those states into political enemies.

Many of the laws that were introduced at the state level were approved when the practice, far from having totally disappeared (the last reported lynching happened in 1964), had dwindled for years, certainly not the laws themselves. The main cause was the public opinion that had slowly developed an acute adverse sensibility toward this practice. At the same time, the support that, more or less explicitly, lynching had received from the press started waning even in the southern states. Even today, the photos of lynchings that took place only as far back as fifty years still provoke in us horror and incredulity. Remembering that page of American history serves a purpose. This is history that for the longest time many tried to erase. Remembering it will help remind us to be vigilant to prevent the horrors of the past from returning, under different guises, even in our time.

---

[66] Cutler, *Lynch-Law*, pp.230-1 and 351-7.

1. THE BEGINNING OF IMPUNITY

1. Eureka, Nevada, 1879.

What happened in Eureka was not, strictly speaking, a lynching. It was, however, one of the very first times the Italian embassy became involved in an episode of public violence and killing of innocent Italians by the police during a labor conflict. The incident contributed to establishing a culture of impunity that in the following years became widespread and protected individuals (in this particular case it was law enforcement agents) who used wholesale violence against Italians, whether they were peaceful citizens or riotous rebels.

On August 18, 1879, a "bloody confrontation [took place] between law enforcement forces and Italian workers on strike in Eureka, Nevada. Five dead, six wounded, several arrests."[1] In his telegram to Ambassador Alberto Blanc, the Italian consul in San Francisco Diego Barrilis added a recommendation: "I sent telegram to Italians recommending calm self-control." This was the beginning of a "tradition" that became the template for subsequent cases of anti-Italian violence, with the consular authorities mostly worried about an explosion of anger.

That Italians could be "hot headed" during labor conflicts was confirmed by Consular Agent Luigi Monaco, who in a telegram from Eureka on August 20 acknowledged: "It is undeniable that our fellow countrymen went beyond the boundaries of legality and acted inconsiderately. At the same time it is demonstrable that the sheriff and his deputies have also abused their authority."[2]

---

[1] ASDMAE, Rappresentanza Diplomatica Italiana a Washington (1861-1901), b. 35, f. 60. From Italian Consulate in San Francisco to Italian Embassy in Washington, August 20, 1879.
[2] Ibidem.

In a follow-up report on August 22, 1879, Consul Barrilis described the context surrounding the clash between police and the strikers who demanded a salary increase: "It was the consequence of the strike organized by Italian and Swiss charcoal-burners in Eureka County, Nevada, following the refusal by mining companies to raise the price of coal by a few cents." The consul was cautious about the true dynamics of the events: "Thus far crucial details have not been ascertained yet. It is still unknown whether the police or the workers fired the first shot." Nevertheless, he mentioned a few details that "nailed" the police. "Only three of the 15 or 16 Italians that were arrested were carrying weapons. This seems to indicate that they did not intend to initiate the violence. It seems, therefore, that Eureka's police acted with unjustified haste."[3]

The results of an investigation were brought to a grand jury in a climate of tension that did not bode well for an impartial outcome. In anticipation of a predictably unfavorable verdict, Consul Barrilis asked the ambassador whether it wouldn't be expedient to consider an intervention by the Italian diplomatic authority "in favor of the victims of those tragic events."[4] In the meantime the Italian community in San Francisco reported diffuse hostility on the part of all other ethnic groups. Shortly thereafter this state of affairs was confirmed. In a telegram Consul Barrilis alerted the embassy about "unrest in the San Francisco colony caused by the Eureka events and by the investigation by the coroner hostile to Italians."[5]

After an investigation on the ground conducted where the clash took place, Consul Barrilis wrote a very meticulous and well documented reconstruction of the events. This is particularly interesting for the description of the Italian and Swiss settlement in this godforsaken area of Nevada: "About 1,500 Italians and 500 Swiss live in the Eureka area. They work in the nearby mountains making charcoal briquettes used by blast furnaces in the treatment of mineral ore extracted from two mines in Richmond and Eureka Consolidated."

---

[3] Idem, August 22, 1879.
[4] Idem, August 22, 1879.
[5] Idem, August 23, 1879.

Work conditions had progressively gotten worse and earnings had plummeted. The consul reported in detail the widespread discontent among mining workers: "This state of affairs has exasperated this peaceful and hard-working population. Instigated by a few leaders, they held two meetings attended by about 500 workers." In the meetings the workers agreed to ask for a higher price for the charcoal they produced. The unrest was caused by exasperation and, allegedly, by "agitators and demagogues" who took advantage of the situation to radicalize the conflict and to lead Italians on the road of lawlessness. "Up to the incidents the workers were acting in accord with legality, but at one point the illegal act began. […] Ill-advised by demagogues and agitators, who are always present in this circumstances, they started organizing armed groups who roamed the mountains to prevent with violence that coal be shipped to the towns."

After the preventive arrests by the authorities of a few potentially dangerous coal-burners, on August 18 the sheriff organized a dragnet aimed at capturing the heads of armed gangs that sabotaged the production and sale of coal. The sheriff was carrying arrest warrants that listed fictitious names since the authorities didn't know the real names of these individuals. After intercepting a group of strikers, the deputies in the sheriff's posse dismounted from their horses and took a crouch-to-shoot position to stop the strikers from advancing. At this point the two versions, the sheriff's and the strikers', begin to diverge. According to the deputies, from the strikers' location, who had previously resisted arrest, a shot was heard being fired, and at that point the posse started shooting in self-defense. The coal-workers, predictably, had a different version, claiming that they did not resist arrest and, most of all, did not shoot at all, neither before nor after the shots from the posse. As a matter of fact, no member of the posse was shot, while there were five victims among the workers, three Italians and two Swiss.

Consul Barrilis collected sixteen sworn depositions from the workers. He found that they all coincided and, consequently, pointed the finger at the police. He also recognized that acts of violence had been committed by Italian miners. "It is undoubtedly true that the Italians acted violently and made threats. It is also undoubtedly true that police officers acted in haste and opened fire against the Italians without warning and without being fired upon either before or after [the first shot.]" Barrilis suggested a solution that in a few years would become standard operating procedure, albeit a humiliating one: close the case asking for an indemnification for the victims' families in exchange for the predictable acquittal of the police officers responsible for the killings. The consul explained the rationale: "Therefore it seems to me that since the culprits may be found not guilty of those criminal acts, they should at least be held responsible for the damage, and forced to pay an appropriate indemnity to the victims' families." Barrilis added a detail that could make a decisive difference if the grand jury accepted the testimony of an Italian. This consisted of "a deposition which could severely affect the position of the police." According to it "one of the deputies in the sheriff's posse [...] before they started out on their patrol, told [the Italian] that he had armed himself because they were going to kill Italians (he used the term *Modok*, the name of an Indian tribe that many Americans use as a derogatory term to refer to Italians)."

The official investigation found the offense not punishable, the first in a long series of cases that in the following years regularly ended with identical verdicts. "The day after the incident, the coroner conducted an investigation establishing that the Italians had been killed by the sheriff posse in the exercise of its legal function." Based on what he had learned by the rumors circulating in the county, Barrilis made the prediction that the acquittal was never in question. The disappointment of the outcome was caused by the criteria of justice, but even more than that, by the fact that these were based on the financial implications for the county. "From what I could determine, conventional wisdom in Eureka has it that the District Attorney will throw out the charges. The reason, commonly accepted, is that if police officers were found guilty, this would entail a major burden for the county for it would be required to pay legal expenses and indemnities."

The consul also mentioned the additional issue of inequality that became crucial in many other cases of anti-Italian violence. Their economic condition made it impossible for them to afford legal representation: "Italians cannot hire a lawyer — Barrilis lamented — since they don't have the means to afford the expense that in this country is enormous." The consul was also worried for the state of frustration and unrest among Eureka's Italians. In theory he was supposed to guarantee the protection of the Italian government, a protection that would never be delivered. "I recommended again to the Italians in Eureka to keep calm, not to commit inconsiderate acts. I reassured them about the support of the [Italian] Royal Government."[6] The verdict of the grand jury that came out a few months later had never been in doubt. "It states that there is no ground for further action against the sheriff and his posse. Moreover, it fully approves of their conduct."[7] This was the first of a long series of cases.

2. VICKSBURG, MISSISSIPPI, 1886

This is the first true case of lynching of an Italian citizen. The events have been reconstructed using a variety of sources, among which are the testimonies of Consular Agent Natale Piazza and reports of local newspapers, both Italian and American. On March 25, 1886, Federico Villarosa, an Italian whose real name was Francesco Valoto, from Palermo, was arrested for the attempted rape of a ten-year-old American girl and was taken to the county jail. The same night the sheriff, after he heard rumors that some citizens were planning to kill the prisoner, tried to transfer him to a different prison under the cover of darkness. On the way to the new location they were intercepted by a group of enraged citizens and forced to retreat. Worried that the rage could degenerate into a lynching, the sheriff contacted the governor of the state asking that he send the state militia to protect the prisoner. The mob was, in fact, dispersed by the militia that reestablished order until the following day. The next evening, however, a group of individuals, "thirsty for hu-

---

[6] Idem, September 4, 1879.
[7] Idem, December 20, 1879.

man blood,"[8] and probably in agreement with the jail guards, took Villarosa from the prison and hanged him from a tree.

The local America press, in particular *The Vicksburg Evening Post* and Vicksburg's *The Commercial Herald*, initially supported and praised the conduct of the sheriff who had prevented a possible summary execution. After the killing, however, they took an ambiguous position, avoiding condemnation of the lynching while reporting the events in a "neutral" tone. To the contrary, the Italian press in the United States and in particular the newspaper with the largest circulation, the New York-based *Il Progresso Italo-Americano*, reacted vociferously, protesting the barbaric lynching: "A man was accused of a heinous crime then summarily strangled by the animal-like rage of the plebes before he could be heard by a judge and found guilty. This man could be innocent, he could be a martyr."[9] The newspaper started an on-site investigation, beginning with the reconstruction of Consular Agent Piazza who from the beginning had raised doubts about Villarosa's culpability, stating: "In reality, I don't believe there is anything true to the accusations." The medical examination of the girl also did not provide any evidence. According to the Italian newspaper, it was a case of molestation related to drunkenness, an extremely serious crime but a far cry from the kind of offense that could justify lynching: "Our unconditional revulsion in front of any act of turpitude toward the innocent prevents us from making excuses for the unfortunate victim's hanging."[10] The next day the newspaper returned to

---

[8] ASDMAE, Rappresentanza Diplomatica Italiana in Washington (1848-1901), b.59, f. 711. From the Consular Agent in Vicksburg to the Royal Consul General in New York, March 30, 1886. According to the newspaper *The Vicksburg Evening Post* (March 29, 1886) the lynch mob was composed of 50-75 individuals.

[9] "Il linciaggio del Villarosa a Vicksburg, Miss." In *Il Progresso Italo-Americano*. April 2, 1886.

[10] The article continues with a salvo against the Irish, the eternal enemies: "This was a most heinous action, worthy of cannibals, in which was present the explosion of the always-present latent rage of the Irish against us Italian." The same article makes an implicit comparison between the purity of Italian and American girls: "Dear God! In America, where little girls are so different from ours that we can say no more…" (Ibidem).

the topic, calling the authors of the lynching "assassins." In this analysis, the episode represented a quantum leap in the ongoing discrimination of Italians. "This dark state of affairs enters a new phase. This is no longer an issue of national honor. It is an offense against humanity that needs vindication." With this the *Progresso* questioned the merit of the type and gravity of the crime, with the opinion that the Villarosa case did not justify that kind of reaction since the specific crime had not been committed. "Even if we accepted the barbaric practice of lynching as a sad American plague that occurs when the people have no hope for the steady and peaceful application of legal justice, we have always seen this measure applied only to criminals guilty of horrible offenses, after they confessed or were found guilty and whose culpability was throbbing and unarguable."

From these premises the accusation of ethnic discrimination emerges: "Perhaps because he was Italian — the *Progresso* fathoms — they wanted him dead, more out of vengeance than for justice." The thesis of an anti-Italian atmosphere was supported by an analysis of the method pursued in the murder, with clues that suggest that the lynchers were aware that they were about to kill an innocent man. "The dynamic of the lynching itself was murky and unusual. [...] Normally a lynching party defies the law with joyful and mocking indifference: better in full sunlight; if it happens at night they light up torches and bonfires around the gallows. [...] In Vicksburg instead they put out the fires choosing darkness." As to "what can be done" about the failure to bring the assassins to justice in a regular trial, the newspaper had no doubts: it is our duty as well as the duty of the consular authorities that represents Italy in America."[11]

The Italian ambassador to the United States, Baron Fava, immediately submitted a protest to the American secretary of state. The complaint was approved by Italian Minister of Foreign Affairs Carlo Felice di Robilant.[12] However, in this case as in all the others of lynching of Ital-

---

[11] "Ancora del linciaggio dell'italiano a Vicksburg, Miss." *Il Progresso Italo-Americano*, April 3, 1886.
[12] ASDMAE, Rappresentanza Diplomatica Italiana in Washington (1848-1901), b. 59, f. 711. From MAE to Italian Embassy in Washington, June 6, 1886.

ians, the culprits remained unpunished. In Vicksburg in particular, after the affair the general attitude toward Italians went from bad to worse. Almost a year after the lynching, *Il Progresso* denounced "the state of chronic anxiety affecting our fellow countrymen who live in that area, where they are the object of constant harassment and degrading insults by a part of the population and in particular by a local newspaper, the *Daily Commercial Herald* that, for reasons we can't understand, has launched a brazen and dishonest crusade."[13]

The atmosphere had become even more tense after the acquittal a few weeks earlier of an American citizen who had killed an Italian, defined by the *Progresso* as "the poor Tironi." The anti-Italian climate was mostly due to the competition for jobs and the fact that Italians were generally willing to accept lower salaries than other ethnic groups. On one occasion, a group of Italian workers passed through Vicksburg on their way to Alabama to build a railroad. Speculations immediately began that "they came to town to compete with the locals for jobs at a miserly rate."[14] *Il Progresso* launched an attack on Italian authorities for the weak or even inexistent protection afforded to our fellow citizens and blamed the local press for creating a discriminatory climate against Italians living in the city "denouncing them to the local workers as worthy of hatred and contempt because they were stealing and usurping jobs at bottom prices, which placed them — sadly — even below the Chinese."[15]

3. Louisville, Kentucky, 1889

What happened in Louisville could be described as a "minor" episode of lynching that went almost unnoticed, even by the Italian authorities. Maybe the reason was the clear culpability of the man involved. The San Francisco newspaper *L'Italia* on June 24, 1889, in a short newsflash reported the events without any sense of alarm, with the plain

---

[13] "Ancora per la difesa dell'onore e per la pace della colonia di Vicksburg." *Il Progresso italo-americano*. April 18-19, 1887.
[14] Ibidem.
[15] "Per la difesa dell'onore e per la pace di una Colonia." Idem, April 17, 1887.

headline "Contractor murdered by an Italian. Killer lynched and brother shot." The newspaper reported the facts that took place in the valley near the Cumberland Gap in a work camp where workers were excavating a tunnel. Antonio Cravasso and his brother were bakers. They sold bread to the workers and they were owed money. They asked G.W. Norwood, a contractor from Birmingham, Alabama, if he could withhold the money directly from the workers' paychecks to repay their debts. The response was negative. The two brothers asked again and, in front of another refusal, Antonio Cravasso shot the contractor with his pistol, killing him. The two brothers were arrested and sent to the Pineville prison. However, as the newspaper reports: "On the way to prison, the enraged citizens grabbed Antonio and hanged him from a nearby tree. As the police continued toward Pineville, a shot was fired and the other prisoner fell to the ground wounded in the back. Needless to say he also died."[16]

Approximately a month later, on August 2, 1889, the diplomatic chargé d'affaires in Washington wrote to Consul General Giampaolo Riva in New York thanking him for "arranging [illegible] from the Governor of Kentucky the report I received from the judge on County Bell concerning the lynching of an Italian in that state." The chargé d'affaires concluded his report with a boilerplate formula of good wishes that wasn't followed by any pressure on the local authority: "I hope that my request for information will encourage the local judiciary authority to pursue legal action against the lynchers."[17]

---

[16] *L'Italia*. June 25, 1889.
[17] ASDMAE, Rappresentanza Diplomatica Italiana in Washington, (1848-1901), b. 59 , f. 734. From Italian Embassy in Washington to Consulate of New York, August 2, 1889.

II. THE GREAT LYNCHING AND THE FALSE LYNCHING

1. NEW ORLEANS, LOUISIANA, 1891

It is the worst episode of mass lynching in the history of the United States, with the death of eleven Italians: three of them were still Italian citizens while the remaining eight had already obtained American citizenship. Some had already been acquitted of the charge of murder. Others had not been tried yet. The episode has attracted the attention of several scholars[1] not just for the gravity of the offense but also because it marked a change in the relation between the Italian and the United States governments. After the New Orleans massacre, the Italian government, caught unprepared to face a diplomatic crisis of this magnitude, became more assertive in demanding justice when similar episodes occurred — although with rather modest results. It was also the only time in history when the Italian ambassador in Washington was recalled, with the diplomatic confrontation continuing on for over a year. Most important for American scholars is the fact that this was the first time that the American government faced the problem of a revision of the U.S. Constitution, forced to do so by the lynching episode against foreign citizens. The constitutional revision was requested by the Italian authorities to ensure the protection of foreign citizens, compelling Congress to take into consideration a variety of legislative proposals.

As to what was at the origin of the lynching, here are the facts. On October 15, 1890, the New Orleans Chief of Police, D.C. Hennessy,

---

[1] For an analytical reconstruction of the case, see R. Gambino, *Vendetta. La vera storia del più spietato linciaggio in America. L'assassinio di massa di emigranti italiani a New Orleans*. Milano: Sperling&Kupfer, 1978.
M.Rimanelli, S.L. Postman. *The 1891 New Orleans Lynching and U.S. — Italian Relations. A Look Back*. New York, 1982.
L. Casilli,."Un drammatico episodio dell'emigrazione italiana. Il linciaggio di New Orleans del 14 marzo, 1891." *Studi Storici Meridionali* Maggio-Agosto 1991, 2.

was found murdered. The investigation focused exclusively on the Italian colony, a community of approximately 30,000 people in a city with a total population of 242,000. The first step was to arrest hundreds of Italians under suspicion of being involved in the crime and, most of all, of belonging to Mafia or the city's "Black Hand." The arrests were conducted indiscriminately, targeting individuals who weren't even remotely connected to the crime or criminal organizations. Worse yet, as Italian Consul in New Orleans Pasquale Corte reported to Ambassador Fava, the investigators applied all sorts of illegal methods to extort confessions and information from the people in custody. These, in turn, later denounced to the consul the maltreatments they had been subjected to. Based on accusations made by the Italian consul, two of the investigators responsible for the maltreatments were put under arrest and properly charged. At the same time, rumors began to circulate about a "vigilance committee" organized or at least "tolerated" by the mayor of New Orleans. Its aim was the elimination at all cost of the plague of Mafia from the city. Faced with the intervention by Ambassador Fava, the governor of Louisiana, Francis Nicholls, gave ample reassurance that the Italian colony was in no danger. As a matter of fact, for a while the situation calmed down, at least temporarily.[2]

The trial against the alleged perpetrators of the crime — later described as a "farce" — ended in March 1891 with the acquittal of the accused, probably caused by the corruption of some of the jury members. The verdict provoked a reaction of indignation in the citizens, triggering an extremely violent demonstration that led to the lynching of the Italians still detained in the city jail.[3]

---

[2] For the entire documentation, see FRUS 1891, pp. 658-63.

[3] In the opinion of a jurist of the period, Augusto Pierantoni, the definition of lynching was limited to very specific cases of popular justice in societies not-yet fully constituted: "The New Orleans massacre did not present the characteristics of a lynching. [...] It lacked the condition of flagrancy, the rudimental forms of a popular jury trial with analogies to the charges and verdicts against the alleged culprit. Instead, it had the seditious character of a violation of individual rights and protections inscribe in the federal constitution and in the constitutions of the individual states." A. Pierantoni. "I linciaggi negli Stati Uniti e la emigrazione italiana." *Italia coloniale,* 1904, 4, pp.446-7.

Copious correspondence was exchanged among the various official agencies in the aftermath of the massacre. It is therefore possible to reconstruct the events with considerable accuracy and shine a light on the unarguable responsibility of the local public authorities and their activity as accomplices, or even as co-participants, in the lynching. The existing documentation covers the exchanges between the Italian consulate and the embassy; the Italian embassy and the ministry of Foreign Affairs; the embassy and the American State Department; and the State Department and the governor of Louisiana.

The Italian consul in New Orleans, Pasquale Conte, followed the case with great participation, zeal and competence although he lacked "diplomatic tact" toward American authorities. While his qualities made him an important point of reference for the majority of Italians, they also led the Italian authorities to the conclusion that he was not suited for his task, since he was too emotional, impulsive and, to some extent, even uncontrollable. The day after the lynching, clearly in a state of shock, he wrote to Ambassador Fava: "I don't have the time to describe the horror of this mass massacre that the disgusting populace, led by the main members of the vigilance committee, committed against defenseless prisoners who had been already acquitted or were awaiting trial."[4]

Among the eleven victims, some were hardly model citizens, not unlike many other Italian residents in New Orleans. The list sent by the Italian Minister of Foreign Affairs, Antonio Starabba di Rudinì, to the Italian ambassador in Washington contained less than glowing information on some of the victims: Loreto Comitis from Navelli had already been sentenced three times in Italy; Antonino Marchese, whose real name was Antonio Grimando, from Monreale, had a criminal record in Italy; Rocco Geraci, from Palermo, escaped Italy with an arrest warrant on this head; Emanuele Polizza, from San Giuseppe Jato, had a reputation as a mafioso, but he had never been sentenced. Some, however, did

---

See also P. Nocito "La legge di Lynch e il conflitto italo-americano." *Nuova Antologia,* s, III, CXVII, Roma, 1891.

[4] ASDMAE, Serie Politica "P" (1891-1916), b. 445. From Italian Consulate in New Orleans to Italian Embassy in Washington, March 15, 1891.

not have a record: Vincenzo Traina, from Contessa, had never been involved in illicit activities, either in Italy or in the United States; Antonio Abbagnato, from Palermo, had a clean record, the same as Girolamo Caruso, from Palermo, Pietro Monastero from Caccamo and Antonio Scalfidi from Patti.[5]

Consul Corte confirmed that some of the victims did have a bad reputation in the city. He also reported the rumor according to which the acquittal had been "bought": "It is indeed true that among the accused there were some very unsavory individuals. It is also true that the evidence presented by the state was contradictory, unfounded or incomplete. To many, these factors in addition to bribes (as the rumors say) must have contributed to the failure of the investigation to bring charges on some of the suspects and the acquittal of others." The lousy reputation of the victims was certainly not a justification for such a violent reprisal, although the consul apparently was not aware of the state of exasperation of the citizenship. To him, the involvement and active role of the urban élite were much more serious, particularly the "Committee of the Fifty." This special commission had been appointed by the mayor to help other local authorities investigate the assassination of Hennessy. "I understand — Corte wrote in a letter to the ambassador — only to a point the irritation of the population and the bloody outburst, but I cannot understand how the educated class could become the leader of such a shameful assassination. And I understand even less how the authorities at all levels, municipal, judiciary, administrative, not only didn't do anything to prevent it, but willfully consented if not actually instigated and helped in carrying it out."

Never before had a lynching been so clearly anticipated and announced. The consul reconstructed the series of messages and signals that explicitly foreshadowed the kind of reaction that would take place in the city. "Starting the evening before, street urchins were shouting and throwing rocks at the vehicles that carried the prisoners, anticipating the more serious disorders that would take place the next day. Violent

---

[5] ASDMAE, idem. From MAE to Italian Embassy in Washington, July 25, 1891.

articles appeared in the evening newspapers, the *Daily States* and the *Delta*, carrying an announcement by the Committee of the Fifty of a rally the next day (yesterday) to repair the verdict. There were no questions as to what means they would use." If the authorities wanted to, it would have been easy to prevent the lynching: "To avoid exposing the prisoners to certain death it would have been sufficient to move them to another location. Yesterday, when at 9:00 in the morning a mob with men armed with Winchester rifles started gathering, it would have been enough to issue an order of dispersal to disrupt the planned massacre."

The consul became more and more alarmed as the hours ticked away. He went looking for the mayor to warn him that violence was in the air — but he had disappeared and was probably hiding somewhere. Sheriff Villere, who was in charge of the jail where the prisoners were kept, and Attorney General Rogers "appeared to be very calm, as if they were cognizant of what would take place later." The governor, in turn, told the consul that he couldn't act without a request from the mayor.

During the long and useless wait for the mayor, Consul Corte found out that a mob had broken down the prison's doors and had already hanged three prisoners. The macabre description of what he saw after arriving at the location continues: "I saw several cadavers hanging from trees. The massacre was over and the crowd was leaving. I returned to the consulate and by the door three black individuals hurled themselves toward me. I had to extract my revolver to keep them at bay. A few seconds later I was joined by Mr. Papini, the consulate's secretary, all shook up and scared. He told me that when he saw a crowd running toward him screaming 'kill the Italian' he escaped by hiding in a storage room."[6]

2. THE EMBASSY REACTS

As soon as he learned the news of the massacre, Ambassador Fava contacted Secretary of State James Blaine, "invoking forceful measures."

---

[6] ASDMAE, idem. From Italian Consulate in New Orleans to the Italian Embassy in Washington, March 15, 1891.

Fava, on orders from Minister di Rudinì, immediately decided to take strong action with the American authorities, submitting a formal protest "against the unjustifiable attitude of the local authority. I invoked forceful measures of protection in favor of Italian royal subjects and I demanded the immediate punishment of the killers, the accomplices and the instigators of the massacre, reserving to the government of His Majesty the right to subsequently request any other reparation that may be deemed necessary."

The inextricable knot of the conflict between Italy and the United States hinged on the formulation of the portion of the U.S. Constitution that contradicts the international treaties ratified by the federal government. According to the U.S. Constitution, the federal government has the authority to stipulate treaties with foreign countries. International treaties, together with the Constitution and the body of federal laws, constitute the supreme law of the land. These binding principles could not be modified by local legislations and the respect of these laws is mandatory for all judges in every state. The principle could not be contested, as confirmed by Secretary of State Blaine to the governor of Louisiana with strong and unmistakably clear words on March 15, immediately after the New Orleans massacre.[7]

As to the application of treaties, the U.S. Constitution guarantees that the states that subscribe to international obligations will automatically provide all the necessary means to ensure that all ensuing obligations will be honored. Article 3 of the February 26, 1871, treaty between Italy and the United States contained a clause that equated the respective citizens, stating: "The citizens of each of the high contracting parties shall receive in the states and territories of the other the most constant security and protection for their persons and property, and shall enjoy to this respect the same rights and privileges as are or shall be granted to nationals, provided that they submit themselves to the conditions imposed to the latter." Italians, therefore, would enjoy the same protection afforded to American citizens without special privileges simply for being

---

[7] See FRUS 1891, pp. 666-7.

foreign citizens. Nevertheless, local public authorities should at least assure the Italian government about their commitment to an effective action of prevention of possible crimes against Italian citizens, with the prosecution of the culprits when such crimes occur. Ambassador Fava was aware of the shame felt by the federal administration as a result of the lynching. "Secretary Blaine reiterated his horror at the events, but he also reminded me, as I expected, that the federal administration, according to the Constitution, finds itself in a very delicate situation vis à vis the authority of a totally independent state with its own legislation, extremely jealous of its prerogatives to the point of not allowing any interference that could infringe on its rights and its autonomy."

The telegram of condemnation publicly delivered to the governor of Louisiana by the secretary of state on behalf of the president of the United States was interpreted by the Italian ambassador as a gesture of respect for the Italian government. "In consideration of the special situation of this country and of the near impossibility for the central power to interfere in the affairs of individual states, the telegram [...] should be interpreted as a proof of deference toward His Majesty's government." In the first meeting between Fava and Blaine, the American minister confidentially mentioned the payment of an indemnification to the victims' families as the easiest way out of the problem. A similar solution had been applied in the case of the lynching of Chinese citizens,[8] and it eventually became the template for future analogous cases. "I should confidentially add that in our conversation the secretary of state repeated several times [...] that a request for indemnification by the families of the three Royal subjects would be favorably received" by Congress.

---

[8] On November 30, 1885, twenty-eight Chinese citizens were lynched in Rock Spring, in the Wyoming Territory, after they refused to participate in a strike. The victims' families received a monetary compensation. See Cutle: *Lynch-Law*, p. 259.

3. ITALIANS IN THE UNITED STATES CRY OUT FOR JUSTICE.

While dismay, anger and humiliation in Italian colonies in the United States were reaching red-hot levels, as was typical in similar cases the recommendation by the ambassador to the consuls was prudence: "Italian newspapers in New York in yesterday's issues published irresponsible articles bound to instigate the colony to conduct reprisals. I thought it expedient to send to the Royal Consul General [in New Orleans] the telegram [...] to recommend to the Italian colony to stay calm and respect legality."[9]

It was certainly true that after the lynching several Italian colonies in the United States had manifested signs of the kind of rage and eagerness to fight that could have easily gone over the edge. At the same time they were experiencing pain, frustration, impotence and fear. Father Giacomo Gambera, a missionary from the Scalabrinian order who was present during the lynching, when confronted by the bewilderment of the New Orleans Italian colony, decided to seek help from the missionary order of Mother Francesca Cabrini: "The state of pain of Italians led me to ask for help from the missionaries of Mother Cabrini."[10] Mother Cabrini in that moment was in Italy, however she immediately acted to give succor to the despondent colony. She eventually arrived in April 1892. Father Gambera urged her to open a school for Italian children, an initiative fully supported by the city's Archbishop Francis Janssens.

Ambassador Fava was very worried about the rage and frustration present in all Italian colonies. In a telegram to Minister di Rudinì, on March 18, he wrote: "Forced to beg Your Excellency to prohibit Royal Consuls from speaking to newspapers." In a "confidential and private" report, the following day Ambassador Fava repeated his apprehension to the minister. After the New Orleans events "an explosion of indignation has taken place in every Italian colony in the country. Telegrams of protest, of rage etc. have inundated and are still arriving to the Royal Lega-

---

[9] ASDMAE, Serie Polica "P" (1891-1916). From Italian Embassy in Washington to MAE, March 16, 1891.
[10] M.L. Sullivan. "Mother Cabrini. Italian Immigrant of the Century." *Center for Migration Studies*, New York, 1992, p. 124.

tion. The Italian newspapers, especially from New York, published special editions and posters inciting the colony to pursue vengeance and reprisals."

Italians did not enjoy a good reputation in the United States and the risk that they would launch into out-of-control vendettas made the situation particularly tense. According to Fava: "In consideration of the seriousness of the situation; of the generally unfriendly attitude toward Italians that are present in this area, (…) in order to avoid very dangerous consequences and in the interest of a rapid solution of the incident between the two governments, it is indispensible to recommend maximum caution to the various colonies."[11]

The proclamation issued by Consul General of Italy in New York Riva to his fellow countrymen followed the same line. On the one hand it showed understanding toward the indignation caused by the massacre, on the other it used reassuring tones to describe the decisive action of the Italian government, and, finally, it stressed the duty of diplomatic personnel in Italy to placate the tension. "We assure you that the authorities of the Motherland are with you and that they share the dismay and pain of your souls, but at the same time they have the duty to persuade you to follow moderation."[12]

The American press, as if to minimize such an extreme action, largely attributed the lynching to the presence of Mafia in New Orleans and all that it was causing to the city. The Italian press, to the contrary, in every Italian colony in the United States that lived in a climate of anxiety and fear, most of all in New York, Philadelphia, San Francisco and Galveston, Texas, denounced the monstrosity of the mass massacre and gave voice to their desperate thirst for justice. In particular the New York-based *L'Eco d'Italia*, in a special edition issued immediately after the news of the lynching on March 14, 1891, came out with the headline *7 Sicilians butchered in New Orleans,* reporting with horror the killing that

---

[11] ASDMAE, Serie Polica "P" (1891-1916). From Italian Embassy in Washington to MAE, March 19, 1891.
[12] "Il Proclama del Console Generale d'Italia, cav. G. P. Riva, on the mournful tragedy of New Orleans." *L'Eco d'Italia* March 17, 1891.

took place following the not-guilty verdict. In the editorial *The Massacre of the Innocents* it stated: "There is no other name for the horrendous massacre of the seven Italians that took place in New Orleans. We are sickened. Our hands shake while writing [...] those poor Italians were innocent [...]. But [...] a ferocious populace rushed to lynch them inside the prison. The wolves found that the doors to the pen had been opened by the shepherds so that the sheep could be slaughtered." The newspaper called immediately for a "mass-meeting against the coward assassins" egging on Italians to actions of reprisal: "Not words, immediate facts! No tears, vendetta!" The newspaper urged for unity, cognizant of the fact that almost all Italian colonies were split internally and very litigious: "There are moments we must set aside misunderstandings, hatreds and anger: there are moments when we must remember we are Italian. As such we urge the *Progresso* and *Colombo* to join with us in a mass-meeting," concluding: "Death to the assassins! Death to the cowards that allowed the slaughter!"

In these moments of extremely high tension, the revelations of the New Orleans consul, Corte, did not contribute to calming the situation. He went as far as *de facto* accusing the state authorities of being responsible for the lynching through public statements that were printed with great prominence by *L'Eco d'Italia* on March 19. First of all the consul took the defense of the mistreated New Orleans Italian colony by the American press: "it is undeniable that the Italian colony is hard working, industrious, frugal and peaceful. Proof of it is the constant requests [for workers] I receive from farmers." He continued with accusations against the "petty politicians" of Louisiana responsible for protecting the worst part of the colony. "This does not exclude the fact that among them there are approximately 100 criminals escaped from Italian prisons, long naturalized American citizens, who are involved in state and city politics. They are protected and taken care of by politicians and with their support many have reached important political positions."[13]

---

[13] "Revelations of the Italian Consul in New Orleans. Louisiana state authorities are guilty." *L'Eco d'Italia* (New York) March 19, 1891.

The references are to the "political" mechanism of naturalization, the right to vote and the involvement in local politics. This is explained with clarity by the successor of Conte, Riccardo Motta, in a report dated May 14, 1892. "Almost all Italian immigrants as soon as they arrive are urged to request American citizenship. Unfortunately, often they don't even observe the waiting period that, according to the law, is required before submitting an application. Rather, with the help of false testimonies, they declare they have already lived here for a year and they are allowed to start the process with an application. At that point they can start voting in elections. This happens in the city of New Orleans where Italians vote as a block under the control of certain politicians, but it also happens in the countryside where plantation owners make them cast votes for their favorite party." Most of the Italians who took the first steps toward American citizenship in reality didn't want to lose their Italian citizenship: "It is a fact that very few of those who submit the initial application, after the required five years of residence complete the process of naturalization. For them it's enough to be able to vote and don't care about anything else."[14]

With regard to the New Orleans lynching, according to the accurate investigation by Consul Corte and his "revelations-denunciations" published by *L'Eco,* in order to understand what happened, it was necessary to trace the conduct of the public authority after the Hennessy assassination. Hennessy was notoriously corrupt and, allegedly, he supported one of the two warring Italian criminal factions in the city. Still, the responsibility of authorities was evident: "If after the assassination the mayor had not issued a proclamation against Italians attributing the crime to them before the trial; and if the authorities had acted more with calm and better judgment, without arresting hundreds upon hundreds of innocent Italians keeping them in prison for days, subjected to abuse and with their possessions stolen — as was proven in front of the grand jury

---

[14] "New Orleans. Rapporto del R. Console cav. Avv. Riccardo Motta (14 maggio 1892.") In "Emigrazione e colonie." *Rapporti di R.R. Agenti Diplomatici e Consolari.* Roma: Ministero degli Affari Esteri, 1893 (462.)

despite the mayor's denials — the mayor would have been supported by all citizens, and especially Italians."

The consul's report continued with a denunciation of the fact that several members of the jury accepted bribes; that it was clear from the very beginning that the trial would end up in a farce; and that the trial represented an opportunity to get rid of a few Italian criminals. "Clearly there existed a faction that was against the prisoners, pushing for a guilty verdict at all cost, for immediate financial interests and in order to justify the mayor's statements declaring that the Italians were guilty, so as to get rid of dangerous individuals. [...] None of this justifies the assassination of impotent prisoners."

The not-guilty verdict reached by the jurors caused an immediate reaction, particularly on the part of the Committee of the Fifty. They called a meeting to decide on counter measures and there could be no doubt about their intentions. Still, it wouldn't have taken much to prevent the lynching: "All they had to do was move the prisoners to a different location."

4. Italy Demands Justice

Minister di Rudinì instructed Ambassador Fava to pursue forcefully a request for concrete reparations that can be summarized in two points: prosecution of the culprits and an indemnification for the victims' families. A simple statement of apology and regret would not be sufficient. These demands were to be conveyed to the secretary of state by Ambassador Fava who, temperamentally, was much more moderate and "diplomatic" than the minister. Minister di Rudinì, although cognizant of the constitutional constraints, expected concrete fact and not just words.[15] The federal government was facing the impossible task of giving a concrete answer to the demands of the Italian government while the Italian American public opinion was becoming more and more "legitimately

---

[15] ASDMAE, Serie Politica "P" (1891-1916). Telegram from MAE to Italian Embassy in Washington, March 19, 1891.

impatient."[16] The convergence of these factors caused the deteriorations of the relations between the two governments. Minister di Rudinì, who in addition to being in charge of foreign affairs was also prime minister, was forced to adopt a hard stance with the American government. In fact, he was under constant attack for being too weak both in Parliament and by a large majority of the press, in particular by newspapers such as *La Riforma* that supported his main political adversary, Francesco Crispi, who had preceded him as minister of foreign affairs. Ambassador Fava, while loyally executing the directives of the minister, was nevertheless supporting a more moderate approach, inclined to giving the American government more time to sort out this difficult problem without excessive pressure from the Italian counterpart. Di Rudinì, in turn, concluded that Fava was actually closer to the positions of Secretary of State Blaine: "I regret that you almost appear to defend the federal government," he wrote in a telegram.[17] The conflict eventually escalated into a long controversy that led to a break in the diplomatic relations and, on March 31, to the recall of the Italian ambassador from the United States — and consequently, of American Ambassador Albert G. Porter from Italy. Current affairs would be handled by the Secretary of Legation, Marquis Guglielmo Imperiali di Francavilla.

The case was amply debated in the press of the two countries. In America it took heavy nationalistic tones, defending against the attempts by a foreign nation to interfere with American policies and legislation. Some publications took a softer line: for instance *The New York Herald* on April 3, 1891, reduced the complex controversy to a matter of misunderstanding and irrelevant misinterpretations of tone and language, under the headline "Misunderstanding between Mr. Blaine and Baron Fava," insinuating that Fava was a bit thin-skinned and that di Rudinì had actually complicated the situation.

A portion of the American press used the episode to push anti-immigration protectionist policies. With the interruption of diplomatic

---

[16] ASDMAE, idem, March 24, 1891.
[17] ASDMAE, idem. Telegram from MAE to Italian Embassy in Washington, March 26, 1891.

relations and the ambassadors' recall a sensationalist campaign of condemnation and ridicule for Italy's requests began, presenting Italy as an aggressive nation determined to resort to military means — if not outright war — with naval operations, thanks to the superiority of its fleet. In reality the Italian government never considered the option of war for obvious reasons related to the respective weight at the international level. No diplomatic document, not even confidential and secret reports, discusses this possibility, not even as a threat. However, the conflict was used by the American press to unify a country that still had deep divisions stemming from the Civil War, with the argument of the need for unity for national defense against a threat from abroad.

The climate kept getting worse with unpleasant episodes like the publication in the *Philadelphia Inquirer* of April 12 of an anti-Italian cartoon. Resorting to the basest stereotypes of Italian immigrants, the cartoon ridiculed by name some of the highest personalities of the Italian government, such as the minister of foreign affairs, the ambassador and the king himself. Di Rudinì was represented as an organ grinder, King Umberto I as a peanut seller with a monkey, Ambassador Fava holding a tin can begging for charity, while Secretary of State Blaine, enraged, upset the peanut cart causing the king to fall down. In a second frame, reacting to Blaine's offense, the king and the minister took out stilettos — the Mafia's typical weapon — getting ready to attack Uncle Sam.[18] The accompanying article mentioned that the king "had become enraged" at a cartoon that "ridiculed His Majesty and belittled the power and dignity of Italy," and that "Italian blood was still boiling."

For Minister di Rudinì the stalled situation created "the most painful impression" that Blaine's conduct was artificial and specious with regard to the Italian request that the culprits be punished and that "he is not giving in to our legitimate demands."

The Italian minister, however, acknowledged that Blaine was right to wait approving an indemnification to the victims' families until after it was demonstrated that the treaty had been violated. In his words "it is

---

[18] "King Humbert Gets Mad." In *Philadelphia Inquirer* April 12, 1891.

repugnant to us to believe that in his mind the violation still needs to be demonstrated. Italian citizens, acquitted by American jurors, were slaughtered inside a state prison, without any provision to defend them. What other evidence does the federal government need to determine the violation of the treaty in which constant protection for the respective citizens was explicitly agreed upon?"

The Italian government acted correctly. It was not up to the federal government to untie the knot of its relations with the States of the Union. The minister continued: "It is now time to end this ungainly controversy. Public opinion, the supreme judge, will point to the correct solution to this serious problem. We affirmed our legitimate right and we will affirm it again: the federal government should evaluate if it is in its interest to leave at the mercy of the individual States of the Union the validity of treaties to which the faith and honor of the entire nation have been committed."[19]

5. THE GRAND JURY CANNOT FIND THE CULPRITS

The grand jury that met on May 5, 1891, drafted a report that acquitted the lynchers, notwithstanding the fact that nobody had been charged, let alone brought to trial. The reasoning was that it was not feasible to put on trial an entire city for acting in such an extreme way without premeditation. Confronted with a verdict that blatantly contradicted the evidence, and the well founded suspicion that some of the grand jury's members had been bribed, the New Orleans newspaper *L'Italo-Americano* on May, 1891, commented: "The verdict reached by the jurors has stunned the citizenship to such a point that suspicions now circulate against some of the jurors, accused of dishonesty in discharging their duty. The evidence presented by the State, according to the grand jury, was overwhelming but the jurors had been corrupted."[20]

---

[19] ASDMAE, Serie Politica "P" (1891-1916). From MAE to Italian Embassy in Washington, April 28, 1891.
[20] "Rapporto del grand jury sul massacro del 14 marzo." *L'Italo-Americano* (New Orleans, LA) May 9, 1891.

Part of the grand jury's report focused on the demonization of the Mafia "sect," depicted at the same time in picturesque and stereotypical terms. The report states: "In order to avoid detection, they choose knives and stilettos as deadly weapons to stab the victims in the chest or the back, to quickly commit the act. Their rallying cry is 'vendetta.'

The ethnic aspect dominated, regardless of the official nationality of the victims, and appeared to dominate the report: "The mafia *caporioni* [big bosses] and many of its members are well known. Some of them, born in this city but from Italian parents, are involved in the vilest activities — and they should be held in eternal disgrace. The largest group is formed by Italians or Sicilians who ran away from their native land, most of the times with fake names, to avoid punishment for crimes they had committed. Others are criminals and bandits rejected by their country who came to New Orleans to enjoy the company of their peers. [...] As of today the Italian consulate has a list of approximately 1,100 Italians and Sicilians known for their criminal background in Italy and in Sicily."

The protection initiatives of the Italian government were considered like a formal duty more than a concrete interest, given the reputation of those individuals: "Hundreds of them now live among us and we have no doubt that the Italian government prefers to have nothing to do with them, rather than being responsible for their protection and their punishment. The character of what is called the Italian colony living in the city and the surrounding area is well known." In condemning Mafia, the grand jury in effect branded with fiery words all kinds of Italian associations, and not only in Louisiana. "Whether it is mafiosi, socialists, nationalists or any other kind; whether they live in New Orleans, Chicago or New York, their gatherings create and instigate seditious sentiments with the manifest tendency to criminal acts that have the flavor of the most brutal betrayal."[21]

---

[21] The text of the grand jury of May 5th 1891, in FRUS 1891, pp. 714-22, translated and delivered to MAE on May 6, 1891, by Consul Corte, in ASDMAE, idem, Serie Politica "P" (1891- 1916).

The day after the grand jury report, on May 6, 1891, Consul Corte wrote an open letter to the foreman of the jury, W. H. Chaffe, which was published by the city's newspapers. He repeated his analysis and conclusions, namely that the killing of the acquitted prisoners happened with premeditation and with the complicity of law enforcement officers. Consul Corte agreed with the jury's analysis about the presence of Italian organized crime in New Orleans, however, he believed it would be very difficult to get rid of them "because, in the majority, they are naturalized American citizens who are supported by some politicians and some authorities." This, in his view, made the lynching even worse: "For the very reason that a large number of criminals live here, I was even more stunned that people were sacrificed, despite the fact that they were good citizens already acquitted or not yet tried."

The hard work of Consul Corte during this affair, his tenacity, the search for justice and his courage in taking personal risks were deeply appreciated by New Orleans Italians, who were accustomed to distant and uninvolved consular authorities. In particular, *L'Italo-Americano*, on May 9, 1891, under the headline "Finally," praised with pride his qualities and his skills in discharging his duties. "In the midst of so many mystifications, lies, errors and contradictions that have been hurled by the authorities and the press at our country and the Italians who live here, a voice of calm and dignity has been heard, effective and authoritative in shedding true light on these sad events. With great pride we honor the courage of our consul, Mr. Corte, who, fully aware he was putting his life at risk, did not hesitate to take action to honor the truth."

With his inquiry Corte had alienated the local authorities to the point that, as he lamented, "I am now threatened by a request for my recall by the United States government."[22] As a punishment for acting openly and undiplomatically in defense of the Italian colony, the consul was "sacrificed" in order to show that the Italian government maintained a conciliatory approach in a matter that could not be closed satisfactorily for both parties. This was confirmed in a message by di Rudinì to the

---

[22] ASDMAE, Serie Politica "P" (1891-1916). From Italian Consulate in New Orleans to MAE. May 10, 1891.

embassy: "Our spirit of conciliation was extended to the maximum possible, to the point that I recalled Consul Corte to get an explanation about his conduct, based only on the doubt that he may not have displayed a totally conciliatory behavior."[23]

The climate in the meantime had become extremely tense and eventually escalated into exasperation with labor conflicts on the docks. Corte provided the first information in a secret report to the minister: "The situation has gone from bad to worse and a catastrophe could occur anytime and nobody can predict who will end up on the losing side. [...] Fruit importers and ship owners, both Italian and American, have made it clear that they want to hire only Italians to unload fruit because they are the only ones who can do the job right. American longshoremen, with the support both explicit and behind the scenes of police and city authorities, want the same jobs and they organized a mutiny, threatening Italians who, in turn, took up arms to defend themselves."

With the precedent of immunity granted to the lynchers, the labor conflict was seen by some as an extension of the previous events, with slogans like: "Who killed the Chief?" Several Italians were wounded, including a woman.

The consul asked that the Italian government send, or at least promise to send a warship, to give heart to the colony in such a delicate moment. Labor conflicts were not the only issues that exasperated the climate made incandescent by the lynching. Another reason was a banking initiative by the consul in favor of Italians: "I believe that one of the main reasons for the irritation of the citizens who belong to the Democratic Party is our role in supporting the creation of an Italian bank where Italians will be able to deposit their savings with the consequence of diminishing the profits of American banks."[24]

---

[23] ASDMAE, idem. From MAE to Italian Embassy in Washington, May 28, 1891.
[24] ASDMAE, idem. From Italian Consulate in New Orleans to MAE, May01, 1891.

6. Diplomacies Face off

The diplomatic confrontation had immediate consequences on the relations between U.S. Ambassador to Italy Porter and Minister di Rudinì. In the course of a meeting about the lynching the two had a heated exchange of opinions on how the respective governments should tackle the issue. In a note to the Italian ambassador in Washington,[25] di Rudinì relayed the positions of Secretary of State Blaine concerning the rights of foreigners, as conveyed by Porter, namely that "foreign residents did not constitute a privileged category."[26] Blaine stated that "the treaties between Italy and America guarantee equality of treatment of Italian and American citizens, and therefore Italians could not be treated in America differently from Americans." Di Rudinì retorted that "this thesis is valid in the abstract, but that in concrete cases it was necessary to demonstrate that American laws allow for the killing of American citizens when they are captive in state prisons."

The main argument put forth by Porter was the same that had been used before with the most restrictive interpretation, namely that American institutions did not allow the federal government to interfere, nor to act in any way against the state of Louisiana. Italy, therefore, could not demand that the United States act in a way that was contrary to its own laws. Di Rudinì, on the other hand, regarded it as unacceptable that the federal government had no responsibility for the action of the States of the federation. "In the face of international treaties this lack of responsibility is patently absurd. If that were the case, the federal government should not have signed those treaties."

At the same time any action by the Italian nation against the state of Louisiana would be regarded as an act of war against the whole United States, and not against a single state. "If Italy supported its demands to the state of Louisiana with the presence of its fleet, we would consider the use of force as a declaration of war" wrote di Rudinì, reporting his conversation with Porter. Porter recognized that "American institutions

---

[25] ASDMAE, idem. From MAE to Italian Embassy in Washington, May 28, 1891.
[26] From Mr. Blaine to Marquis Imperiali, FRUS, 1891, p. 685.

were somehow defective," however he claimed that "the established practices of the country allow for changes in the institutions" only through a complex and lengthy process of constitutional review. The Italian minister, from his position, considered that perspective to be unsustainable "in the face of the civilized world."

The most disturbing information Porter mentioned in non-official conversations was that while in America the massacre caused horror, American citizens were irritated because the Italian government had dared criticize the conduct, the delays and the institutions of that country. Porter "added that American public opinion was angry at what was regarded as a threatening tone by Italians, meant to put pressure on the United States without allowing for enough time to debate the matter." Di Rudinì, on his part, defended the moderation of the Italian government who went as far as recalling Consul Corte from New Orleans.

Chargé d'affaires in Washington Imperiali after receiving di Rudinì's report about his conversation with Porter, replied with a refutation of the American ambassador's statements. In particular he rejected the claim that American public opinion had reacted in horror to the lynching, "a statement [...] that is perhaps in line with the wishes of the United States representative, but that is nevertheless incorrect." Imperiali claimed instead that the greatest part of American public opinion had accepted, if not outright approved, the massacre without horror: "The general belief was that the victims of the March 14 massacre were all a gang of thieves and assassins who belonged to the Mafia that had been terrorizing the city of New Orleans, with infiltrations in the justice system. Therefore, while they objected about the means, the majority of the public cheers at the results from the bottom of their heart."

Imperiali was absolutely convinced that the United States had this deeply rooted conviction that summary executions were a necessity.

"I formed this conviction after reading both the New York newspapers as well as those published in other states; and after hearing with my own ears statements and declarations made by people who belong to the most enlightened strata of society and the world of politics; and from comments by other diplomats who mentioned this fact with horror."

Imperiali continued comparing the actions of he American government to that of a "vast and permanent electoral agency," in the sense that every move by their members was determined by a calculation on "the interest of the party they belong to and the number of votes that any decision will affect at the next presidential elections." This was the source of an attitude that didn't take into account the effects these barbaric acts had on the international level. "The near universal condemnation by civilized Europe against the United States didn't produce any result because for the American masses the rest of the world does not exist; and also because the press abstained from reporting what was said against their government on the other side of the Atlantic."

Imperiali believed that, realistically, the most Italy could extract from the Americans was a presidential recommendation to Congress for a vote in favor of an indemnification for the victims' families. As to the prosecution of the culprits, he recognized that the United States Constitution did not give the federal government any leeway for independent action. Only the Republican Party was in favor of a constitutional change, since "traditionally it always supported the centralization of powers in the federal government with a limitation of autonomy by the states." According to Imperiali it would be unrealistic to expect a constitutional change, even if it were supported by the president. In Congress it would have unleashed a wave of the most intense nationalism "because *Americanism* would revolt against an Executive Branch's recommendation resulting from criticisms by a foreign power against the American Constitution." Moreover, it was unthinkable for Imperiali that "the House of Representatives, which in the next Congress will have an overwhelming Democratic majority, would allow a vote on a proposal that goes against all the most fundamental traditions and principles of the party, and, on top of it, directed against Louisiana, which is its core."

Imperiali's opinion with regard to re-establishing diplomatic relations with the United States, after the recall of the Italian ambassador and consequent American countermeasure with Porter, was that Italy had no choice but to go first, despite the fact that it was the "offended" nation. The unequal power of Italy and the United States and their different political weights at the international level didn't leave any other solution. Imperiali commented that "the federal government is aware that Italian interests in the United States are much larger and more important than American interests in our Kingdom, therefore it won't change course and it will expect that Italy makes the first move toward re-establishing normal relations." This was the epitome of paradox: the nation that suffered the offense had to endure the arrogance of the government that should have made reparation for the injury. "On one side the Kingdom is in the right to demand reparation for the offense against His Majesty's subjects. On the other side the United States government, in part because of constitutional restraints and in part for ill will based on electoral pressure, refuses any reparation, or, at least, responds with a kind of silence that, to my eyes, looks like contempt or at minimum callous indifference."

The American government, in the meantime, stood firm in its position while skillfully manipulating both the pro- and anti-govern-ment press. It thus succeeded in "exciting the people against Italy, in distorting the calm, reasonable and dignified attitude of the Royal Government, claiming that the recall of Ambassador Fava was an arrogant, menacing and provocative act." In this context, Imperiali explained Blaine's words to Ambassador Fava before he was recalled: "I do not recognize the right of anybody to give orders to the people of the United States." "The secretary of state knew full well that those words would be made public. It would show that the government of the Republic defended the rights and dignity of the American people, with the certainty that the news would be received with great favor by the public, drenched in *Americanism*." The decision of the Italian government to close the diplomatic incident was interpreted by American public opinion as a defeat for Italy, with general approbation for the federal government. "There was unbound satisfaction when the newspapers published the lofty and composed dispatch with which Your Excellency declared the intention to put an end to this unrewarding controversy. 'They are retreating. We achieved victory!' Such was the cry repeated in all the newspapers, while the president and Mr. Blaine were congratulated by the leaders of the two parties."

Imperiali also reported a sentence pronounced by Blaine to Fava that revealed the full-blown arrogance of the federal government: "I am perfectly indifferent to the opinions about our institutions abroad; I cannot change the Constitution and even less violate it." These words "unfortunately reflect the exact way of thinking of the overwhelming majority of American citizens and the legal stand of the government."[27] The reference to the reactions abroad was related to the condemnation that the New Orleans had received in Europe, especially by France and Germany. Austria was more tentative while the newspaper *The Times* of London almost sided with the American government.

7. THE CONTROVERSY IS APPROACHING CONCLUSION

Mr. Imperiali, following a similar strategy as Ambassador Fava, tried to moderate the intemperate attitude of Secretary Blaine. He explained that since Italy didn't intend to declare war on the United States — as was clear it wouldn't — it was forced to present the issue in such a way that would compel the federal government to accept it.[28] It wasn't easy, however, to resolve the conflict in a manner that would give an honorable way out. Minister di Rudinì was willing to move in that direction only on the condition that "Mr. Blaine demonstrates that he wants to resume negotiations." The Italian government had put forth two requests: prosecution in a federal court and indemnification. Di Rudinì believed he was right to think that "Washington is giving some hints that it is backing away from the rejectionist position adopted thus far." In private conversations the Italian minister had sensed the possibility that "the next Congress may debate the question of the federal government's powers over the governments of individual states, thus patching the legislative gap that was observed on the occasion of the tragic New Orleans events." This initiative, together with the payment of an indem-

---

[27] ASDMAE, idem. From Italian Embassy in Washington to MAE, June 15, 1891.
[28] ASDMAE, idem. From Italian Embassy in Washington to MAE, August 25, 1891.

nification, could be acceptable to Di Rudinì as long as the proposal came from the United States and not from Italy.[29]

It took a year from the date of the lynching before the complex controversy could be solved. A major step forward came from the president of the United States, Benjamin Harrison, who in the State of the Union Address to Congress on December 9, 1891, explicitly condemned the New Orleans massacre. It was only in March 1892, however, that Minister di Rudinì declared his satisfaction with the decision of the federal government that "in accepting the friendly suggestion of Italy, will order the ambassador of the United States in Rome to return to his post, and will accept the appointment of a Royal ambassador to the United States, thus fully reestablishing diplomatic relations on the most friendly basis."[30]

Although the diplomatic crisis was over, the Italian government was not completely satisfied, since it had not been able to succeed in having the culprits brought to justice. The president of the United States proposed for the families of the victims indemnification of 125,000 francs, emphasizing the fact that the offense had not been caused directly by the United States. "Although the offense was not inflicted by the United States, the President considers it a solemn duty and a great pleasure of the national government to pay a satisfactory indemnification."[31] Ambassador Fava upon returning to Washington was solemnly received with Secretary Blaine by President Harrison to make official the solution of the diplomatic incident.[32] One year later, on May 19, 1893, the Italian legation in Washington was elevated to the rank of embassy, similarly to those of France and the United Kingdom.[33]

---

[29] ASDMAE, idem. MAE to Italian Embassy in Washington to, September 25, 1891. The Italian government took another step toward resolving the crisis by suspending a ban on import of pork meat from the United States. See ASDMAE, idem. From Italian Embassy in Washington to MAE, October 23, 1891.

[30] ASDMAE, idem. From MAE to Italian Embassy in Washington, March 18, 1892.

[31] Mr. Blaine to Marquis Imperiali, Washington, Apri 12, 1892, in FRUS 1891

[32] ASDMAE, idem. From Italian Embassy in Washington to MAE, May 23, 1892.

[33] F. Loverci. "Il primo ambasciatore italiano a Washington: Saverio Fava." *Clio* 1977, 3.

The gap in American legislation remained an open problem, but now that the diplomatic incident was closed, the debate could begin without giving the impression it was due to pressure from the Italian government.

A bill was introduced the Senate in May 1892 by Senator Joseph Dolph. The Dolph Bill proposed an expansion of federal powers over the jurisdiction of individual states concerning the protection of foreign citizens. In the debate in the Senate, the bill was attacked harshly for being unconstitutional. Ambassador Fava, in a sad tone, wrote: "There have been numerous and strong attacks against this proposal, considered to be unconstitutional. [...] No decision has been made and no vote has taken place." A few voices in the Senate remarked how the position of the federal government vis-à-vis other nations was unsustainable. Senator John Morgan, for instance, demonstrated "how precarious was the position of the United States, forced by its own laws to publicly declare its inability to execute treaties that involve the honor of the whole nation."

The process for a change in the Constitution required the approval of both branches of Congress, something that was far from being assured. In any case the procedure would require a long time, in that it concerned the autonomy of the states. Fava was legimately proud to have been the first ever to raise such an important issue: "Italy will forever have the honor of having being the first to force the attention of this government on a defect of the law concerning its relations with foreign nations."[34]

8. THE COLONY AFTER THE LYNCHING

In the years after the lynching of 1891 the Italian colony went through a period of relative calm, without major episodes of criminal activity, giving the impression that the times when the colony was a synonym for the Mafia were over, to the point that the lynching, horrible as it was, could almost be considered an aberration. Alfonso Lo Monaco, a medic who worked on ships covering the Palermo-New Orleans route,

---

[34] ASDMAE, idem. From Italian Embassy in Washington to MAE, May 25, 1891.

of the 1891 lynching wrote: "It was a shameful excess, unworthy of a highly civilized people such as the Americans which will never be justified nor will have the excuse of mitigating circumstances. On the other hand [...] the Italians of New Orleans had committed so many crimes that the massacre was almost like the inevitable retribution for the situation."

The analysis of the situation by the Italian medic, however, was too optimistic when he stated: "Right now, for our good fortune [...] the dark times of blood and crimes are long gone and [...] the evil plant of Mafia which had very deep roots in this city has apparently been uprooted completely from American soil." This contrasted with the assessment made by the consul who had reported time and again about the involvement of a part of the colony in the dirtiest political deals of the city. Lo Monaco instead was saying that "moreover, the Italians resident in New Orleans had the common sense not to get involved in the political affairs of the country, to stay completely away from public life, thus avoiding political hatred and enmity."[35]

There still was a suspicion, rather justified, that the acquittal of the Italians charged with the Hennessy murder had resulted from the corruption of the jurors, a suspicion that was not erased for years and that resurfaced from time to time in similar circumstances. The Italian Consul in New Orleans, Giuseppe Saint Martin, twelve years after the lynching in a confidential note to Italian Ambassador Mayor expressed skepticism in consideration of the facts that, over time, the New Orleans Mafia had made substantial progress in the city. In discussing the very recent and very suspicious acquittal of some Italians accused of murder, in which the involvement of local Mafia or "Mano Nera" was apparent, Saint Martin wrote: "This acquittal represents a danger for the future. It is universally known that the New Orleans lynching was the consequence of the acquittal of the murderers of Chief of Police Hennessy, an

---

[35] A. Lo Monaco. *Da Palermo a New Orleans*. Roma: Loescher, 1897 (152-4.)

acquittal that was obtained in a way similar to the recent one, and that was considered a success for Mafia."[36]

The criminal element tied to the Mafia inside the Italian colony of New Orleans, if anything, had become stronger and was now causing serious concerns. Twenty years after the 1891 lynching it was so widespread that the Italian Ministry of Foreign Affairs felt compelled to give the consul general instructions for a rather unusual policy, namely, that he not involve the consular representation in the affairs of the local colony. On the occasion of yet another crime inside the colony, namely the murder of Giorgio Di Martino by Vincenzo Moreci, the minister sent the consul a confidential note that stated: "I don't believe it is the case to get involved for such criminals, except if it turned out that American authorities made mistakes in the investigations that led to the incrimination of the culprits."[37]

The following year, during the Second Convention of Italians Abroad, held in Rome in June 1911, a special committee that had been created in New Orleans for this purpose, published a report with the title *Juridical and Social Considerations on Italian Emigration to the United States and in Particular to Louisiana*. The speaker was Luigi Scala. It is a very interesting analysis conducted inside the colony, yet it kept an elitist distance from the very Italians that were being discussed. Scala explained their conduct without even minimally identifying himself as part of them. Among other things, concerning the Italians' bad reputation in the region, he took the defense of his fellow countrymen but at the same time he felt compelled to acknowledge the existence of a festering problem in the community: "The moral situation of Italians in Louisiana has been painted with dark colors. True, in the past there have been painful events, that are now almost forgotten, and because of them the general population has developed a veiled negative attitude toward our nationality, something like contempt for the anonymous crowd, that is basically hostility. [...] Some of this may be caused by the low eco-

---

[36] ASDMAE, Consolato di New Orleans (I versamento), b. 1. From Italian Consulate in New Orleans to MAE, March 2, 1903.
[37] ASDMAE, idem. From MAE to Italian Consulate in New Orleans, August 1, 1910.

nomic condition of our emigrants and the frequency of violent crimes that most of the times go unsolved due to the despised penchant for *omertà*."

Once again, the criminal activities of a few were causing damage to the majority of the virtuous Italian subjects of the colony, giving the opportunity to the racist public opinion and the xenophobic press to launch heavy attacks. "The nefariousness of a few criminally minded repeat offenders that often remain unpunished gives the impression of a large number of dangerous felons and raises fear in the public opinion, and not just in Louisiana. It is easy to lose sight of the fact that they constitute a small amount of trash among a multitude of good people, like wilted roses in a bush in full bloom. When this happens, a part of the inimical press whose anti-scientific defense of the purity of races boggles the mind, hurls inconsiderate insults at our entire community. The same can be said for our self-avowed enemies, who drag down to their level the crowd who, otherwise, would be indifferent. The few drag along the many." In an implicit comment about lynching that sounds almost like a justification, he added: "All this is to be condemned. However, if we reflect that human nature is such that in moments of rage it goes overboard and cannot distinguish between the innocent and the guilty, we can understand this momentary phenomenon."

Addressing the echo that those events caused in Italy and the disgust for the discrimination suffered by Italians, the speaker denied that they were facing a generalized phenomenon. "In Italy some expressed loud disdain claiming that Italians are kept below Americans on the social ladder. It would be wrong to conclude that this is the prevailing sentiment. Rather, these are opinions that vary depending on the moment, the place and the individuals." In part it seems as if Scala justified the sense of aversion toward Italians. This comes through when he describes their primitive living conditions. "We can't deny that our emigrants ignore basic hygienic practices; that in the case of an epidemic they don't allow health inspectors in their houses; and that they often renounce buying even necessary items despite the fact that they can afford them. Can we then really blame Americans who in such cases feel repugnance?"

One of the reasons why the Italian race was considered inferior was its familiarity with black people. There were also cases where Italians lived with women of color: "Take the case of a barber: he will shave both white and black clients indifferently, because he does not feel toward blacks the innate repugnance that Americans in southern states feel. As a consequence, white people will avoid going to this barber and his clientele will eventually be only blacks and Italians. No other citizen of the village, whatever race he may be, will patronize this business. Italians do not have toward black people the same semi-hostile attitude harbored by Americans, whose revulsion for people of color is an aspect of historical tradition. Italians treat black people with more familiarity than the natives. Indeed, sometimes they live like husband and wife, sometimes publicly. This is taken as an insult against the white race and leads to threats against their lives, and intimations to leave town." There are considerable differences between life in the city and in the countryside. "In the countryside, where Italians are a minority, these differences are even more evident. It is less so in areas where Italians constitute a strong group, if not the majority of the local population."

Prejudice was not based exclusively on ethnic reasons but also extended to economic rivalry. Scala's paper continued: "People who come here to compete for bread with the established populace, must insinuate themselves step by step. The process of penetration at first is antagonistic: they will suffer some shoves and will have to swallow a few hard words."

On the topic of the common slur *dago* used for Italians "it has penetrated so deeply into the population that it appears often in the mouth of many people who don't use it as a taunt." Scala could not see a realistic and feasible solution to this situation. He believed that a patient wait was the only alternative. "Of course the remedy would be for them to protest individually and collectively every time they hear [dago] so as to stop this habit, most of all when it is meant as an insult. They should also consider adopting the moral and financial boycott of those filthy blasphemous mouths. With time, justice will be done."

For Scala it was both positive and inevitable that second-generation Italian Americans would obtain American citizenship — as they usually did. With a touch of national and even racial pride, he judged favorably the result of the mixing of Italian and American blood. "These new generations in whose veins Latin blood runs, will combine the genius and adaptability of our race with the steady acumen and robust ideals of this land. They will become active agents for good in the multifaceted aspects of American social life." An example could be found in the undeniable economic success of the Italians of New Orleans. "In New Orleans the Italian community, which is more or less 15% of the population, owns no less than 10% of the city's real estate."[38] These data on the economic level reached by the Italian colony were confirmed by Gerolamo Moroni, the consular agent in charge of the immigration office in New Orleans. In an article he wrote: "We can assert with confidence that among the Italians of New Orleans, poverty is unknown. Indeed, many are comfortable and a few are extremely rich. The strengths of the colony are its spirit of solidarity, sobriety and thriftiness."[39]

Despite their economic success and their increased political might, capital executions of Italians continued to be a source of entertainment for the state's citizens for quite some time. In 1924 six Italians, who had declared their innocence until the very end, were condemned by the courts for killing the American owner of a restaurant in Independence, Louisiana, in the course of a robbery. The execution by hanging, on May 9, 1924, in Amite, in Tangipahoa Parish, was attended "by a crowd of thousands of people from the farthest towns in Louisiana."[40] It was a sensational trial, with appeals that went on for three years, and one that from the beginning was liable to cause unrest, especially by the Ku Klux Klan. In order to prevent troubles, the National Guard filled the moat around the prison with water "as a precautionary measure against the

---

[38] Scala, *Poche considerazione giuridiche* (17-23.)

[39] G. Moroni. "La Louisiana e l'immigrazione italiana." *Bollettino Emigrazione*, 1913 (510.)

[40] "Le sei esecuzioni capitali nella Tangipahoa Parish." *Il Progresso Italo-Americano* May 10, 1924.

possible attempt of an attack by fanatical members of the Klan. It was known, in fact, that the Klan was celebrating the execution of six foreigners."[41]

9. SEATTLE, WASHINGTON, 1892

The Seattle lynching never happened. Not only that, it wasn't even attempted. However, the story kept the local press, the Italian consulate in San Francisco and the embassy in Washington very busy for a couple of weeks. This suggests the presence of a climate of ethnic tension, suspicion and fear exacerbated by the New Orleans lynching the previous year. It was in fact considered possible that a similar event could happen again.

On June 17, 1892, the American press, and most of all the Seattle newspapers, gave detailed information about the lynching on June 13 of four Italians and the probable execution of four more. The latter ones were accused of murdering their boss, a Norwegian named Nelson, at a railroad work site for the Montecristo line in Skagit County. One of the Seattle newspapers placed the episode in the context of a conflict caused by the working conditions of Italians. According to the unspoken rules of ethnic hierarchy, Italians were discriminated against and they were assigned only the worst and heaviest tasks, namely the pick-and-shovel jobs, while "white" workers were in charge of the excavation. The reason for the discrimination was that "Italians and Chinese aren't considered part of the white race. Italians had living quarters separate from those of whites."

In the work camp it was normal for everyone — including non-white workers — to carry weapons. "In the camp there are about 175 Italian workers against no more than 50 white men. Anybody that is minimally familiar with railroad work camps is aware that every man in an isolated place like this carries a weapon." Regardless, the stereotype of "hot-headed" knife-carrying Italians returned in the same article, as if Italians were the only ones to go around armed: "Almost every Italian

---

[41] Ibidem.

carries a knife and some have a revolver at the ready."[42] The newspaper's report with the reconstruction of the dynamics of these events was rich of details. Indeed, the following day, June 18, it reported an editorial from the Rome newspaper *La Tribuna* demanding that the Italian government present a protest to the United States government.[43] A few days later, however, the whole story was revealed to be completely fictional.

On the basis of the information sent to him by the San Francisco consul, Ambassador Fava, who had just been reinstated after the restoration of diplomatic relations between the two countries, immediately contacted "unofficially" the President of the United States Harrison, asking him to urge the governor of the state of Washington to take action.

Only on June 20, the same newspaper recognized that the news had no foundation in reality: "No men were lynched." The retraction came from John Orsolini, back from the camp where he had taken seventy Italians. In his opinion the hoax served to "excite anti-Italian prejudice."[44] To the contrary, one of the company's officers, eye-witness to the incident, explained that the story had been invented to scare away foreign workers from the camp and send them somewhere else. He opined that the news, on top of being false, was also implausible given that there were 270 Italian workers and about forty workers of other nationalities. Had such an episode taken place, Italians, being the majority, would have reacted immediately. The Seattle newspaper on June 27 took the words of the company's officer and made them its own: "The 270 Italians would have rebelled in mass and would have taken vengeance for the death of their fellow countrymen."[45]

Ambassador Fava, already on June 21, in his report to the ministry rushed to deny the credibility of the rumors about the lynching.[46] Yet

---

[42] "A Murder Avenged. Four Italian Assassins Hanged in the Woods." *The Seattle Press-Times* June 17, 1892.
[43] "The Story Is True. Four Italians Lynched at Monte Cristo." Idem June 18, 1892.
[44] "No Men Were Lynched." Idem June 20, 1892.
[45] "It Was a Fake." Idem June 27, 1892.
[46] ASDMAE, Serie Politica "P" (1891-1916), b. 357. From Italian Embassy in Washington to MAE, June 20, 1892.

the doubt was still in the mind of the consul general in San Francisco, Bianchi, who on June 24 was doubtful about the truthfulness of the retraction, and waited until July 5 before writing to the embassy reporting that all his doubts had been put to rest.[47]

---

[47] Idem. From Consulate General in San Francisco to the Italian Embassy in Washington, June 24 and July 5, 1892.

III. NOT ONLY THE SOUTH: IN THE WEST

1. Denver, Colorado, 1893

In strict legal terms the victim of this lynching episode was not an Italian citizen, but only for the reason that Daniele Arata, the son of immigrants from Liguria, had already been naturalized American. The case, nevertheless, fits with the category we are investigating since his legal status had no relevance whatsoever for the executors of the crime who, for all intents and purposes, considered the victim an Italian.

Based on the facts reported by the local Italian press and the Italian Consulate, Daniele Arata was the owner of the Hotel Italian and the annexed saloon in Denver. He was an alcoholic, and during a drunken rage in a minor dispute he killed a patron, a well-known war veteran. According to the classic lynching ritual, Arata was forcibly taken from the county jail by a very large mob and almost immediately hanged from a tree. Then, his body was torn to pieces. The Denver-based Italian newspaper *Roma* published a comment about the "demise of a demented man" in a story that detailed the mauling inflicted to the cadaver, under the headline: "The macabre dance of blood. The party and picnic of hyenas and jackals."[1]

There was no way for the authorities to stop the mob. Nevertheless, the Denver newspaper *Rocky Mountain News* condemned the inefficiency if not outright complicity of the police. The rebuke was rather unusual since, generally, the American press in this type of circumstances took an ambiguous stance, often even justifying the action: "The police did not behave appropriately. The police department and the sheriff's office showed themselves completely unable to keep peace. The authorities were in possession of complete and immediate information on the strong

---

[1] "L'assassinio di Werwatta Street." *Roma* (New York) July 29, 1893.

resentment present in the city and could have taken proper measures to prevent the tragedy that has fallen on Denver."[2]

The Italian Consul in Denver, Nicola Bruni Grimaldi, in his report voiced his worries about the safety of the community and tried to dissuade the local Italian community from going to the cemetery en mass, except for the victims' close relatives.[3] Minister Fava, on the basis of the information he had received that the victim was no longer an Italian citizen, explained his decision not to take action in a note to the Ministry of Foreign Affairs in Rome that placed the episode in the larger context of the area's economic crisis and the competition among ethnic groups: "For the record, I shall add [...] Arata would not have been lynched if his crime had not taken place in this particular moment: the closing of silver mines and connected industrial plants has caused an economic crisis. Consequently, a whole population of unemployed and disgruntled workers converged onto Denver looking for ways to survive and it is now keeping the capital under the threat of violence and plundering."[4] Three convicted felons were arrested under the suspicion they were the leaders of the lynching horde, but nothing ever came of it.

Italian traveler De Riseis a few years later left an important analysis about Italian immigration to Colorado. With aristocratic disdain he described the quality of the Italian specimens who emigrated to this land and their awful relations with Americans. After visiting Consul Bruni Grimaldi, De Riseis wrote: "In the waiting room I saw a small crowd of bad characters, mostly unemployed southern laborers; [...] usually it is the worst ones who come all the way here to Colorado looking for jobs that are getting progressively more rare." The writer's conclusions weren't exactly glowing: "There is very little to expect from these knife-wielding drunkards who constitute a large part of our colonies."

And here is his explanation, if not justification, of the lynchings: "Everywhere, the colonies that bear the name of Italy are hated by Amer-

---

[2] "Arata Lynched." *The Rocky Montain News* July 27, 1893.
[3] ASDMAE, Serie Politica "P" (1891-1916), b, 591, f. 430. From the Consulate General of Italy in Denver to MAE, July 31, 1893.
[4] Idem. From Italian Embassy in Washington to MAE, August 3, 1893.

icans who always look with suspicion to these throngs of dirty people, quick with their knives and ready to work for low wages: these are three things that Americans all over America cannot stand. This is the source of the persecutions, the special laws and the *linciamenti*, a word that tragically has been Italianized and has entered the common language due to deadly recent episodes." De Riseis's judgment about Americans and American justice wasn't any kinder. About the Arata lynching of 1893 he wrote: "Of course, once popular rage decreased, the authorities didn't really give much thought to punishing the *linciatori* of Arata. [...] This is America." Americans, in fact, according to De Riseis, are two-faced: the individual, honest and respectable; and the collective, violent and ferocious: "And yet, if you bring together a mass of the people that seem so sweet and meek, you will find crowds of ferocious *linciatori* and enraged *politicians*."[5]

2. WALSENBURG, COLORADO, 1895

Walsenburg was a prosperous coal mining camp of a little more than a thousand people in Colorado where a large contingent of Italian workers were employed. On March 11, 1895, the dead body of a beer maker, Abner J. Hixon, was found. The Italian Lorenzo Andino confessed immediately and was taken to the local jail in town. In the course of the investigation eight other miners were arrested. Four of them were released for lack of involvement, while for the remaining five the arrest was confirmed. These were: Pietro Giacobini, Stanislao Vittone, Antonio Gobbetto, Francesco Ronchietto in addition to Andino. They were escorted to the Walsenburg prison by two deputy sheriffs. On the way to Walsenburg, a posse of five or six people stopped the convoy and started shooting at the Italians on the spot. Vittone was immediately killed, Ronchietto and Andino were wounded. The other two managed to escape. Giacobini was found four days later, exhausted but still alive. Gobbetto also was saved. The first night in jail, in the middle of the

---

[5] G. De Riseis. *Dagli Stati Uniti alle Indie.* Roma: Ripamonti e Colombo, 1899 (39-45).

night, a group of six or seven people, armed and masked, after avoiding detection by the guard, entered the prison and killed the two Italians.

Immediately the Italian ambassador contacted the American secretary of state and the governor of Colorado requesting protection for the Italians living in that county, receiving assurances to that effect by the authorities.

Ambassador Fava, once again, lamented "the serious difficulties encountered by the federal government in enforcing and implementing the various clauses of international treaties in the states of the federation." In fact, despite the good intentions of the federal government to resolve the constitutional conflict that had emerged after the New Orleans lynching "no legislative action has been taken [...] probably because of the extreme jealousy of the states for everything that concerns their autonomy, as recognized by the Constitution."[6] The need for the federal government to solve this question involved relinquishing powers that belonged to the states to the federal government. A part of the American press intervened in the debate showing a preoccupation about possible future crises with foreign nations, and raising the issue that the indemnifications decided by Congress for the victims of lynchings were paid for with tax money from the entire population, and not charged to the state responsible for not preventing the lynchings "perpetrated by outlaw elements in some small village."[7]

The Italian newspaper of San Francisco *La Voce del Popolo*, facing this new episode of violence, reacted in much stronger tones, giving voice to the great worries that all the Italian communities of America were experiencing. The newspaper insisted on the constitutional anomaly in the relations between federal government and individual states that -- after the New Orleans lynching -- had resurfaced and was creating

---

[6] ASDMAE, Serie Politica "P" (1891-1916), b, 605, f. 517. From the Italian Embassy in Washington to MAE, March 14, 1895. The correspondence between the Italian Embassy and the State Department is in FRUS 1895, pp. 938-956.

[7] "Our Treaty Relations. Serious Difficulty in Maintaining Them With Foreign Governments. Legislation Necessary to Give the General Government Power to Protect Foreigners in the States." *The Evening Star* March 14, 1895.

difficulties in the diplomatic relations between Italy and the United States. The newspaper wrote: "The President of the American Union represents the entire nation with foreign powers. However, he has no jurisdiction of sorts over the individual states that compose the Union itself. Therefore, he is entitled to demand accountability from foreign governments concerning any offense suffered by an American citizen on their own territories. At the same time he can dodge the very same accountability claiming that the constitution does not allow him to undermine in any way the autonomy of individual states."

The newspaper encouraged an improbable constitutional reform and openly challenged the existence of the fundamental tenet of reciprocity in the relations between Italy and the United States: "In concrete terms the present situation destroys the most important clause of the international treaties in effect between the United States and other nations, namely reciprocity. [...] It is simply grotesque" — the newspaper added — "that the head of the nation represents the whole while he does not represent its individual parts. His representativeness is, therefore, simply an illusion."

The San Francisco *La Voce del Popolo* wasn't very optimistic about the outcome of investigations to identify the lynchers. The newspaper realistically maintained that "nobody has any delusion about the outcome of those initiatives. Even in the remotely possible case that the offenders may be found and be put to trial, no jury in Colorado will be impartial enough to produce a guilty verdict against them."

The solution of indemnifications for the victims' families was also not taken for granted, since it was fraught with formal complications. "The president's cabinet in Washington has already informally communicated that the indemnifications awarded in the New Orleans case cannot be regarded as a precedent, since it was approved by President Harrison only as an international courtesy toward Italy, as a charitable gesture for the survivors of the unfortunates who had been killed by the crowd." When the indemnifications were awarded the motivation issued by the federal government did not acknow-ledge any responsibility in the events that took place. According to the newspaper "There is no explicit acknowledgment of a right. To the contrary, the United States government insists in rejecting any responsibility in this matter."

Once again the Italian press was forced to push the Italian government and its foreign representatives to demand that the federal government respect international treaties, and not just in terms of "indemnity-charity." The *La Voce del Popolo* rhetorically asked: "Is the Italian government, presided over by Francesco Crispi — a self-proclaimed jealous protector of national dignity abroad — going to accept once again a solution that does not solve the fundamental issue between the two nations?"[8]

The most important issue still awaiting a resolution, before the Italian government could start the official procedure, concerned the victims' citizenship. The investigation revealed that Ronchietto and Vittone had filed only the initial application for naturalization. The remaining three were still "fully entitled" Italian citizens. The simple act of initiating the process for naturalization, according to Ambassador Fava, did not mean that the applicants had acquired the full title of American citizens. This was the claim that, in every occasion, American authorities were trying to make. The ambassador objected that "this [American] government wants to consider as American citizens foreigners who receive the first acknowledgement of application for citizenship, without waiting for the five-year period required by law for full naturalization. The [Italian] Royal Government has always argued the opposite thesis, ruling that Royal subjects, from the time they receive the first papers to the moment they obtain full American citizenship, not even for a moment lose their status as Italians."[9]

The governor of Colorado must have concluded there was some ground in the suspicion that the two deputy sheriffs and the prison guard in Walsenburg had cooperated or at least had not prevented the lynching of the Italians. He was immediately cleared of suspicions and a reward of a thousand dollars was posted for information leading to the arrest of the culprits. This was the highest reward allowed by the Fun-

---

[8] "Il Linciaggio di Walsenburg," *La Voce del Popolo* (San Francisco) March 18, 1985.
[9] ASDMAE, idem. From the Italian Embassy in Washington to MAE, March 16, 1895.

damental Statutes that Colorado had ever posted. With this in mind, Consul GiuseppeCuneo wrote to the ambassador: "This leads me to suspect even more that the local authorities are complicit in the massacre of the Italians, as rumors circulating in Walsenburg claim."

Consul Cuneo had interviewed Giacobini after he had been found. He discovered that "at Bear Creek Bridge they were attacked by only one person and the two deputy sheriffs did not put up any resistance."[10] In addition to the well-founded suspicion of neglect or complicity by the local authorities, the governor's zeal was also in response to the direct intervention — defined as "exceptional" by the Italian news agency Stefani[11] — of the president of the United States. Ambassador Fava confirmed this suspicion, stressing that the local authorities were responsible for not preventing the lynching. In his messages to the Italian minister, to the secretary of state, and, through the consul, to the governor of Colorado, he wrote: "I count fully on your impartiality and justice for the fair solution of this grave affair." Already anticipating the outcome of the dispute, Fava wrote that "for mutual convenience I want to initiate an additional procedure for a possible request of indemnification in favor of families of the lynching's victims."[12]

The governor of Colorado's determination to find the authors of the lynching was for naught. However, his conduct — aside from the fact that he was just doing his job — was so unusual and unexpected that the Italians of Colorado decided to acknowledge his action with an award: "The Italian colony of Denver has resolved to present to the governor of this State an artistic parchment to show its appreciation for his interest and impartiality in the ill-fated Walsenburg affair."[13]

One year after the lynching the culprits were yet to be found. The verdict of the grand jury, relayed to the Ministry of Foreign Affairs by

---

[10] ASDMAE, idem. From the Consulate General of Italy in Denver to MAE, March 21, 1893.
[11] Agenzia Stefani, March 17, 1895, n. 66.
[12] ASDMAE. idem. From Italian Embassy in Washington to MAE, March 27, 1893.
[13] ASDMAE, idem. From the Consulate General of Italy in Denver to the Italian Embassy in Washington, February 19, 1896.

Ambassador Fava, consisted of a very cold statement: "Three Italians and one American on the night of March 12-13, 1895, were killed by unknown assailants. Therefore, there is no ground for continuation due to lack of evidence."[14] Ambassador Fava, "deeply saddened by the outcome of this trial," obtained reassurance by the secretary of state that he would prod Congress to award an indemnification to the Walsenburg victims' families. A few months later Congress approved a reparation of $10,000 to be divided in five parts among the families of the three dead and two wounded men.[15]

An essay by Conrad Woodall puts forth an interpretation of the Walsenburg lynching that challenges its classification as such. Not accidentally the title of his article uses the word "massacre" instead of "lynching."[16] Woodall questions if the act was approved by the local authorities with their complicit attitude; if the cause of the lynching was the nationality of the victims; if other political or union-related reasons contributed to the outcome. The author, rather, attributes it to a "primitive" socio-economic context typical of "frontier justice." "Those deaths — according to Woodall — seem to match what in an infelicitous expression J. Cutler would call a frontier community."

Woodall rejects the interpretation of the slaughter as a form of xenophobic defense, "a typical nativist reaction against a frightened minority of immigrants that threatened to take over the community." The census shows that in 1900 there were only 163 Italians in the area. Woodall denies that the nationality of the lynching's victims had even a minimal role in the episode. He claims that in those circumstances any other eth-

---

[14] ASDMAE, idem. From the Italian Embassy in Washington to MAE, February 19, 1896.

[15] See *Indemnity to Heirs of Italian Subjects Killed at Walsenburg, Colo.*, Department of State, Washington, June 12, 1896, n. 129, in FRUS 1896, p. 422. See also from the Ministro di Grazia e Giustizia e dei Culti, to MAE, October 12, 1896, in ASDMAE, idem.

[16] See C. Woodall. "The Italian Massacre at Walsenburg, Colorado, 1895," *Italian Ethnics: Their Language, Literature and Lives*. Proceedings of the 20th Annual Conference of the American Italian Historical Association, Chicago, Illinois, November 11-13, 1987, Staten Island 1990 (297-317).

nic group would have been subjected to an identical treatment. "The Walsenburg lynching was an isolated event. Belonging to any ethnic group would have represented a problem in those circumstances." The author, rather simplistically, seems to reduce everything to a problem of poor linguistic communication. "The Italians were paying the price of a strong linguistic barrier; […] they didn't have the necessary tools to confront the enraged population."

Concerning the behavior of local authorities, Woodall denies an active role for not preventing the lynching, attributing their behavior to incompetence or indifference or insensibility. "Beyond the loss of lives," the author writes, "the failure to investigate promptly may have been caused by wrong timing, incompetence, inexperience, or by the crudeness of the citizens and the sheriff of Walsenburg."

According to Woodall, the hypothesis that the lynching took place in the context of political or labor fighting has no credit. "Being foreigners contributed to the killing of Lorenzo Andino and his co-national, but there doesn't seem to be any element to show that their involvement in political or labor struggles played a role."[17]

This hypothesis is plausible. Consul Cuneo as well in his reports to the embassy made no mention of a context of labor competition among ethnic groups which, in several other cases of lynchings, played a direct role, as recent historical studies have shown.[18]

---

[17] Woodall, "The Italian Massacre" (312-3).
[18] Higham. *Strangers in the Land: Patterns of American Nativism, 1860-1925* (91).

IV. IN THE OLD SOUTH

1. Hahnville, Louisiana, 1869

On August 5, 1896, in Saint Charles, not far from New Orleans, the Italian Lorenzo Salardino killed an American citizen named Jules Gueymard and wounded his friend Robert Espenard. Salardino was arrested immediately. The New Orleans newspaper *The Daily Picayune* reported that rumors of an impending lynching were circulating.[1] The following day the newspaper talked about the "innate brutality" of the assassin, implicitly giving legitimacy to a killing that had not yet happened. "It is feared that Lorenzo Salardino will be taken away from public officers and hanged on the public street as a warning."[2] On August 8, an angry mob went to the nearby jail of Hahnville to take possession of the alleged assassin along with two other Italians, Salvatore Arena and Giuseppe Venturella. These two had been imprisoned previously and they were awaiting trial for the murder of a certain Joaquin Roxino, an accusation that later would be found to be baseless. The three Italians, all awaiting trial, were hanged by a group of masked men. The most important local paper did not write a single word condemning the event, hiding behind an apparent neutrality while defining the lynching "a protest against the methods of Mafia." No condemnation appeared against the mob either, nor towards the authorities responsible for the *de facto* protection of the accused in this climate of pre-announced tragedy.[3]

The representatives of the Italian government, who immediately understood the enormous gravity of the triple lynching, had to face a series of substantial and formal obstacles. First of all, they found that a climate

---

[1] "Assassinated in St. Charles." *The Daily Picayune* August 6, 1896.
[2] "St. Charles Decides Against a Lynching." Idem August 7, 1896.
[3] "Trio Lynched in St Charles." Idem August 9, 1896.

of fear dominated the county where the Italians lived. This had the effect of hardening the community's penchant for reticence, something already seen in other circumstances that made the work of finding the truth even harder, also in view of the fact that there were strong doubts about the honesty of the work done by local police authorities. The Acting Consul of New Orleans, Carlo Papini, wrote to Ambassador Fava apologizing for his delay in sending information on the case. "Many of the people who knew the victims and could have given the information I sought were totally negative. Some even let me know they were not willing to come to the office unless they got paid for their statements."[4]

The Italian Embassy and the State Department embarked on an epistolary exchange accompanied by a series of meetings in the attempt of solving the problem of lynchings of Italians that had become all too common. The starting point was the treatment resident foreign citizens were entitled to in the United States. After the killings of Hahnville, Ambassador Fava briefed the minister of foreign affairs about the procedure that the Italian government should follow and the steps that the American Constitution allowed the federal government to take: "In those cases, it is prescribed that the federal government has to request the individual state to establish the facts, first of all if the victims had already become naturalized American citizens. If the answer is positive, the American government does not recognize the right of complaint to any foreign government by any naturalized citizens. If, however, the victims of lynching were still foreign citizens, the government would remind the authorities of the state where the crime took place about the clauses of the existing treaties concerning the protection to which the resident citizens of friendly nations are entitled, and urges those authorities, in case they have not taken care of it already, to take all measures necessary for the identification of the lynchers, and for handing them over to the magistrates in charge of prosecution. The Department of State, moreover, becomes actively involved with Congress, which is solely responsible for legislation concerning expenditures, to award an in-

---

[4] ASDMAE, Serie Politica "P" (1891-1916), b. 623, f. 629. From the Italian Consulate in New Orleans to the Italian Embassy in Washington, August 14, 1896.

demnity to the victims' families. None of these latter measures are executed by the secretary of state until he has received the reports from state authorities, with the result of the investigation confirming the foreign nationality of the lynching's victims."

The crucial issue, once again, was the relation between federal government and the states of the Union. The ambassador concluded: "Until the Constitution of the United States stays as it is and the protection of foreigners in all the states of the Union is a federal responsibility, the federal government will have no choice but to continue on this path, urging the individual states to investigate, capture and turn over the offenders to the courts while at the same time applying pressure to prevent the recurrence of lynchings." The only viable solution for all the cases appeared to be reparation money to the victims' relatives. The federal government "always lobbies Congress for the approval of an equitable indemnity for the victims' relatives."[5]

In the case of Hahnville, the governor's report on the lynching took a long time to complete and, consequently, the secretary of state was delayed in starting the procedure for compensation. When the report finally arrived from Louisiana, the secretary of state forwarded them to Ambassador Fava, commenting that the investigation's findings were "very disappointing."[6] The documents confirmed that the grand jury's verdict was identical to those of all the other lynching cases, declaring the impossibility of further action against unknown individuals. Fava, more resigned than surprised, wrote to the minister: "Based on the investigations of the two magistrates, the facts match the reports that appeared in the newspapers; that the coroner could not find any leads about the lynchers; that the jurors at the end produced the usual verdict that the lynching was committed by unknowns; that this bloody episode was the result of the intense indignation caused by the assassination of Mr. Geymard. According to the widespread rumors his murder was blamed on Salardino with the help of the other two; that this massacre

---

[5] ASDMAE, idem. From the Italian Embassy in Washington to MAE, August 22, 1896.
[6] Mr. Adee to Baron Fava. Washington, August 28, 1896, in FRUS 1896, p. 403.

was an explosion of violence that represents a stain for American civilization." The verdict excluded the nationality of the three Italians as a determinant factor: "The fact that other Italians in other prisons were not molested, shows that the nationality of the three victims was not the motive for the massacre."[7]

Four months after the slaughter the question was still unresolved, even after the secretary of state had sent a special agent to New Orleans to investigate the event. In a message to the secretary of state, Ambassador Fava contested the findings of the special agent.[8] Arguing against the preconceived notion of guilt on the part of the three Italians, Fava reminded him that "the fundamental principle of law and justice in all civilized countries, and in no country practiced as scrupulously as in the United States, is that every person is presumed innocent until he is found guilty by a legitimate court." Fava mentioned another recent case that took place in New Orleans, where it turned out that a certain Rocco Bonora, threatened with lynching, had nothing to do with the crime he was accused of. He emphasized that also in the case of the two Italians lynched in Walsenburg, accused of murdering Roxino, the clues were flimsy at best: this was indirectly demonstrated by the fact that the judge had set a very low bail for the two. The only murders with plenty of evidence, according to Fava, were those perpetrated by "cowardly assassins who without any resistance from the authorities, were practically encouraged by the certainty that the investigation would be cursory and ineffective, as indeed it was, and murdered three defenseless Italians whose safety should have been guaranteed by this Country's justice system."

Fava, in his accusation that the investigation was prejudiced from the beginning, claimed that the envoy of the federal government simply gave cover to the responsibilities of the local authorities. "The statements

---

[7] ASDMAE, idem. From the Italian Embassy in Washington to MAE, August 28, 1896. The verdict sent by the governor of Louisiana to the secretary of state, in FRUS 1896, pp. 403-4.

[8] The report by the special agent in Mr. Olney to Baron Fava, Washington, November 27, 1896, in FRUS, pp. 407-12.

by your special agent about the lynching, despite the fact that they tried to justify the local authorities and exonerate them from any fault, actually confirm instead their unjustifiable neglect. In fact, the agent reports that when the news about Mr. Gueymard became public, the excitement was so high that the crowd that had gathered openly talked about lynching. The emotion was so intense that the sheriff had to threaten to shoot the first person who touched the prisoner. The threat of lynching was so real that, the same night, he thought about hiding Salardino in the woods. Nothing could demonstrate more effectively the turmoil and agitation of the crowd." Fava's accusations against the sheriff for his lack of will to prevent the lynching become more and more hard-hitting and articulate. "Despite all this, the sheriff, instead of taking the prisoner to a remote location, safe from the threats on his life, decided to take him to Hahnville, to dismiss three days later the prison guards and to hide prudently somewhere where he could not be found, nor informed in time of potential attempts, thus abandoning the victims to the mercy of the assassins who were keeping an eye on the prison. Such a strange coincidence! He abandoned the prisoners the very same day, and just a very few hours before the slaughter! It would have been impossible to facilitate any further the lynchers' plans. There is just as much co-responsibility and cooperation in omission as there is in commission."

Fava's denunciation did not spare the way the investigation was conducted: "It is evident that nothing was done to find the culprits. It is true that the grand jury met and waited for the assassins to turn themselves in, but since, with good reason, they didn't show up, the grand jury was adjourned after condemning the lynching! No detective was assigned to the case. The police did nothing to find them. The district attorney could not collect any information that could lead to discovering the lynchers because no serious, courageous or even partial attempt was made to this end." The special agent sent by the federal government was also targeted for criticism. Fava believed that "this person tends to justify the insufficient actions of the civil and judiciary authorities of Louisiana."

Once again, the secretary of state attempted to pass the three Italian citizens for naturalized Americans, raising the doubt of whether the Italian government had the right or duty to act against the United States government. The latter claimed that the three victims had already received the first naturalization papers; that they had voted in the state of Louisiana; that, by residing in that state, they demonstrated they had no intention of returning to Italy; that they did not contribute to the Italian nation. Moreover, by violating the Italian laws about mandatory military service and participating actively in the public life of the state of Louisiana by voting, they had become full-status citizens according to the Constitution and the laws of Louisiana as interpreted by the Supreme Court of that state. To the contrary, Fava's thesis insisted on the "principle that United States naturalization can only be accorded exclusively by Federal Laws, and not by state laws" adding that "the universally accepted doctrine is that the sole declaration of intention does not confer citizenship."[9] Once again, this case ended with the pseudo-solution of an indemnity to the victims' families in exchange for the failed capture of the culprits. On July 8, 1897, the Senate voted to allocate $6,000 to the three families, in accordance with the standard "fee" of $2,000 per lynched man.[10]

Approximately a month and a half later, on August 24, 1897, the *New York Herald* published the news that "a black man from Hahnville, Louisiana, confessed to the killing of the old Roccina [Roxino], for whose murder [...] two Italians, Arena and Venturella, together with Salardino, were lynched on August 1896."[11] The news was confirmed by New Orleans Consul Papini: the black man, named Creole, accused of numerous murders and hanged on January 1898, was found guilty of one of them, but not of the Roxino's. A secret report sent by the new Italian Consul in New Orleans to the Italian Embassy two months after

---

[9] See Baron Fava to Mr. Olney, Washington, December 31, 1896, in FRUS 1896, pp.413-8. Copy in ASDMAE, idem.

[10] See Mr. Adee to Baron Fava, Washington, July 30, 1897, in FRUS 1897, pp. 353-4.

[11] ASDMAE, idem. From the Italian Embassy in Washington to MAE, September2, 1897.

the death of Creole, contained blood-chilling details on the torture that the "drunken and savage crowd," "those feral beasts in human form" inflicted on the Italians who, to the very last minute, continued to proclaim their innocence.[12] The worst aspect was the secrecy that the public authorities kept even after the truth was discovered. The consul concluded that "the judiciary authorities after becoming aware through Creole's confessions that the unfortunate Arena and Venturella were innocent, unable to repair the dastardly deed, decided to cover everything up at all cost." Considerations of political expediency, primarily the fear of reactions by Italians in the county, likely led the sheriff to prohibit Creole from confessing the homicide in front of the judge, in exchange for we-don't-know-what."[13]

The Hahnville case marks the last time that Secretary of State Richard Olney used the argument that a foreign citizen who had applied for naturalization automatically became a U.S. citizen and, therefore, lost the protection rights of his native country, yet could still be awarded an indemnity by the federal government. In the Tallulah lynching that came a little later, in 1899, the federal government established once and for all the principle that a foreigner could not be considered a citizen of the United States until he had received the final official papers with the formal notification.

---

[12] Here is the description of how the two Italians were tortured before being killed: "A noose was tied to the neck of each one, while the other end of the rope was looped around the branch of a tree. The rope was pulled and let go so that the feet of the Italians were suspended in mid air or were lowered to touch the ground just before they would die. As soon as the tortured became conscious again, those feral beasts in human form forced them to confess their crime. This torment was repeated several times." In ASDMAE, idem. From the Italian Consulate in New Orleans to the Italian Embassy in Washington, March 30, 1898.

[13] Ibidem.

2. Tallulah, Louisiana, 1899

Tallulah was one of the worst cases of lynching: five Italians were massacred after being accused of attempted murder. The complicity of the local authorities was brazen, as was the local press's. This explains the very harsh attitude of the Italian Embassy, at least initially, and the enormous echo in Italy and in the United States.

The various versions of the facts are generally in agreement: a goat belonging to an Italian, Francesco Difatta, used to enter the bordering yard of a certain Dr. Hodges, the county's doctor and coroner. Eventually, on July 20, 1899, this caused an argument, started by Dr. Hodges. Giuseppe Difatta, Francesco's brother, came to his help and shot the coroner causing a non-lethal, superficial wound. A crowd gathered and the two brothers for self defense barricaded themselves in the house where the third brother, Carlo, was, together with two other Italians, Rosario Fiducia and Giovanni Cerami. When the sheriff arrived he arrested three of the five Italians, who "did not resist arrest despite the fact that they were armed, like everybody else in those places."[14] Carlo and Giuseppe Difatta managed to escape arrest by hiding out somewhere else. In the course of the night, a mob of over three hundred armed people removed the three prisoners and hanged them from the trees in the prison's courtyard. Still not satisfied, they started looking for the other two. They found them and they hanged them in a slaughterhouse nearby. Four of the five Italians were originally from Cefalù, in Sicily, while Cerami was from Tusa, in the province of Messina, also in Sicily. They were working in the fruit and vegetable trade and they had reached a respectable economic position.

The local American press, once again, took a complicit or conniving position. The only exception was the *Evening Post* of Vicksburg that maintained there was "no valid reason for the mass lynching of Italians" and that "this lynching, similar to what happened in New Orleans a few

---

[14] "Il linciaggio di cinque italiani a Tallulah, La." *L'Italo-Americano. Gazzetta Quotidiana della New Orleans* July 22, 1899.

years ago, is motivated only by an outlaw mentality and by prejudices against foreigners."[15]

The grand jury, once again, drenched in the worst and most trite Italian stereotypes, declared that the five Sicilians had formed a conspiracy to kill the doctor. After a "diligent investigation" they claimed the people responsible for the lynching could not be identified. This seems to be rather unbelievable in a place like Tallulah where, according to *L'Italo-Americano* "barely 400 people live and where everybody knows everybody else and where, if there was the will, the culprits could be found easily. Unfortunately, sad previous experiences teach us that NEVER in any case of lynching, the killers have been arrested and punished."[16] The same newspaper, the following day, commenting on the lynchings, defined Louisiana as the "classic land of this superior form of civilization," thus casting blame on the entire population: "The lynching minority enjoys the complicity of the majority of the citizens asleep. Has it ever happened that a jury denounced the names of the members of a lynching mob? Has any lyncher ever been punished? And yet, just one example of full justice would be enough to wipe away the lynching habit."[17]

Italian *chargé d'affaires* in Washington, Count Giulio Cesare Vinci, moved immediately to contact Secretary of State John Hay, who revealed embarrassment and probably even shame for what happened and, as usual, promised total commitment to act in order to solve the case as soon as possible.[18] The Italian consular agent in New Orleans, Natale Piazza, was put in charge of an investigation, with the help of one of the editors of the newspaper *L'Italo-Americano* who had been deputized by the consulate. The investigation's goal was to verify the nationality of the victims and, in case they turned out to be Italian citizens, the sequence of events. It became immediately evident that it would be impossible to

---

[15] *The Evening Post*, July 21, 1899.
[16] "Il linciaggio di cinque italiani a Tallulah, La." *L'Italo-Americano. Gazzetta Quotidiana della New Orleans* July 22, 1899.
[17] "Il linciaggio di cinque italiani a Tallulah, La." Idem, July 23, 1899.
[18] Correspondence between the Italian Ambassador and Secretary of State Hay on the Tallulah lynching, in FRUS 1899, pp. 440-66, and in FRUS 1900, pp. 715.36.

gather credible testimonies about the facts. Piazza wrote: "It is impossible to get any *affidavits* about the crime because there are no longer any Italians in that place and it would not be expedient or prudent or effective to rely on Americans, who are openly hostile toward our nationality."[19]

Piazza sent to the Italian consulate in New Orleans a report containing an accurate review and scrupulous reconstruction of the events, showing that the coroner was responsible for the initial argument, as well as for the silence of the witnesses afterwards. The consular agent was skeptical that the sheriff could be impartial in correctly reconstructing the events, "because after washing his hands of the affair, he doesn't want to take the chance of ending up the same way our co-nationals did, unless the authorities forced him to do so and granted him immunity from prosecution and relocation in exchange for revealing the names of the culprits."

Based on personal impressions, the consular agent described a tangible climate of hostility toward Italians: "I was forced to notice that the people who received us were collectively hostile toward the dead" and that on that particular day "the killing mob acted as if they smelled in an instant the wish of an immense vengeance." With regard to the "origin of such a heinous act, committed by a savage populace with the approval of the entire white population of Tallulah" Piazza thought it could be found in "first, racial hatred; second, the jealousy of the town's merchants who didn't like the fact that the few Tallulah Italians were doing pretty well in their business to the detriment of the locals' interests; third, the opposition to allowing Italians to vote. It is possible that the local power factions were competing for the three Italian votes that could effect the outcome of an election, since the total electoral body is composed of approximately 150 votes."

The only hope, according to Piazza, was the intervention of the governor of Louisiana: "It would be desirable that in the epistolary exchange between the Royal Government, the Embassy and Your Excellency [the

---

[19] ASDMAE, Serie Politica "P" (1891-1916), b. 656. From the Italian Consulate of New Orleans to MAE, July 26, 1899.

Acting Consul of Italy in New Orleans, Papini], the governor be made aware that his intervention is needed to obtain the immediate incarceration of the culprits which may be possible with the arrest of those Law Enforcement Officers who have acted as accomplices of the assassins, and are in any case unworthy of the their titles. Action of this kind would greatly gratify the national sentiment so badly offended by this vile lynching, compared to which all precedents fade."[20]

The reconstruction of the lynching by the majority of the American press, not just the local newspapers, was falsely neutral, reporting a white-washed version of the facts and abstaining from judging the crowd's behavior.[21] Some newspapers, though, presented the Italian victims, and indirectly Italian immigrants as a whole, as rogues and malefactors, thus justifying between the lines the lynchers' initiative as the only defensive measure available to the community.[22] One voice that sang outside the choir was *The Daily Item* that directly blamed the coroner, accusing him of provoking the confrontation, thus dismantling the thesis of a conspiracy to kill him.[23] It was clear, in fact, that Giuseppe Difatta shot and wounded the coroner only after he saw the coroner was about to shoot his brother. New Orleans's *Italo-Americano* denounced the version published by the *Times-Democrat* that justified the lynching as "the only manner possible to secure white supremacy." For the Italian newspaper, there was very little hope that American justice would do its course: "The administration of justice is in the hands of friends of the lynchers [...] who are completely sure of their impunity."[24] The mass of elements accumulated led *chargé d'affaires* at the Italian embassy in Washington, Count Vinci, to the conclusion that the massacre was related to the competition for jobs between Italians and Americans: "Never

---

[20] ASDMAE, idem. From Consular Agent Piazza to the Acting Consul of the Italian Consulate in New Orleans, July 29, 1899.
[21] See *The New York Sun* and *The Washington Post*, July 23, 1899.
[22] See *The Daily States*, July 1899.
[23] See *The Daily Item*, July 26, 1899.
[24] "Un'asserzione coraggiosa sul linciaggio di Tallulah," *The Italo-American* July 27, 1899.

was a lynching more atrocious and unjustifiable, with the traits of a despicable criminal act. The goal was to get rid of foreigners whose business undermined Tallulah's residents."[25]

3. REACTIONS IN THE UNITED STATES

A part of the American public opinion and the press openly took sides against the lynchers, even if with rather questionable arguments. The progressive periodical *Harper's Weekly*, for instance, used as aggravating factor against the lynchers the fact that the victims, although Italian, conducted themselves like "civilized" Americans, as they had accepted the lifestyle of their community: "All the Italians spoke English, had adopted the dress style and the habits of Americans and wanted to become American citizens." However, the writer placed the episode in the context of the conflicts between blacks and whites in the area of Madison Parish — the location of the massacre — where black people were the overwhelming majority of the population without even minimally sharing in the political and economic power. "It is the most black area of the United States: in a population of 16,000 people there are only 160 white families. There are 20 blacks for every white and in some areas the ratio is 1 to 100. Nevertheless, the entire power is in the hands of whites. They own all the land and every other property. They are the only ones who can vote and sit on juries. They elect all the administrative officers and control all the affairs of this area." In such an explosive situation of

---

[25] ASDMAE, ivi. From the Italian Embassy in Washington to MAE, August 6, 1899. The event had wide echo in Italy: there was a parliamentary debate in addition to large coverage by newspapers. In the same year a ballad was composed by a "cantastorie" [street performer]: *I cinque poveri italiani linciati a Talulah* [sic] ("The Five Poor Italians Lynched in Tallulah"): "I sing those poor lynched / Who honest and hard working/ Because their name was Italian/There was no piety for them....Oh Italian youths / lower the flag half mast/ and onto the vile sickening mob/ Unleash your darkest vengeance!" The text is in E. Franzina, *Dall'Arcadia in America. Attività letteraria ed emigrazione transoceanica in Italia (1850-1940.)* Torino: Edizioni della Fondazione Giovanni Agnelli, 1996 (101.)

conflict, crimes committed by blacks and the lynching of black people were rather frequent.

Italians found themselves in the middle of the conflict between whites and blacks, with the unwelcome role of "uninvited third party," difficult to classify, and compared to the image of a bat, half rat and half bird.[26] The most interesting part of the article deals with the problems facing the white community at the arrival of Italians, namely their "placement" in the extant rigid ethnic and social hierarchy. This was further aggrieved by the familiarity that Italians displayed toward blacks: "When the first Italians arrived in Madison a few years ago," — the article states, — "they represented a problem for the white population. Like a bat, they were difficult to classify and this was made even more difficult by the fact that they dealt mostly with black people and were socializing with them almost as if they were equals."

Consequently, they couldn't really be classified as *white*, although they were not black. Relations with them were a problem. In the end, it seemed more "natural" to place Italians at the same level as blacks. Therefore, Italians who dared assault or kill a white man did not deserve a trial but a lynching, just like black people. The article explains: "At the end it was decided that they should expect the same kind of justice reserved to black people who assault or shoot or kill a white man in Madison: no trial, lynching. The white people who govern and administer Madison are not willing to let Italians join their own ranks."[27]

Count Vinci complained to the federal government, which in turn pressured the governor of Louisiana. However, the ambassador didn't think this would be enough to even raise hope about a positive outcome in this complex episode. He reported his skepticism in a letter to Minister Visconti Venosta "so as not to feed too much hope in the effectiveness of that pressure." The specificity of the lynching made it exceedingly difficult, if not outright impossible, to ascertain the facts: "Given that

---

[26] About the complex "color" placement of Italian immigrants in the United States, see F. Fasce, "Gente di mezzo. Gli italiani e gli altri." *Storia dell'emigrazione italiana*. 1, *Arrivi*. Roma: Donzelli 2002. pp. 283-43.

[27] N. Walzer. "Tallulah's Shame," *Harper's Weekly* August 5, 1899.

this is not an isolated murder but a collective crime perpetrated by the entire citizenship of a village, it is natural that the solidarity for the crime is able to mount a resistance that both constitution and laws did not anticipate."[28]

A new case, the "Delfina case" arrived a little more than a month after the lynching to exacerbrate the tension, in a climate that was saturated but not yet satisfied with the blood already spilled. It was another threat of lynching in the same place. The lynchers found out that a brother-in-law of the Difattas, Giuseppe Delfina from Cefalù, totally extraneous to the previous events, had moved to the county. They resolved to complete the job of exterminating Italians. Fortunately, a friend of Delfina caught wind of the plan and was able to alert him giving him enough time to gather his family and find safety by crossing the Mississippi River. However, he had to abandon everything, his store, his land and his business. He was compensated for the financial damage only two years later, as we will discuss later in this book.[29]

The federal government, in the face of the strong protest by the Italian government for the frequent recurrence of violent episodes against its citizens, sent a special agent from the Department of Justice to lead an official investigation in Tallulah's lynching.[30] The news was reported by the news agency Stefani[31] as a great success of the Italian government: "The decision to start this investigation is given great importance in that it recognized the principle that the federal government can intervene — as the Italian government pressed it to do." The wire was picked up by the *Tribuna* di Roma that considered the decision more a necessity for the federal government than for the offended party: "an act of justice that seems more necessary for the Government of the United States than

---

[28] ASDMAE, idem. From the Italian Embassy in Washington to MAE, August 9, 1899.
[29] On the "Delfina case" see FRUS 1900, pp. 715-8. See also "Attempted lynching in Tallulah against another Italian family." *Il Corriere della Sera* September 20-21, 1899.
[30] See FRUS 1900, pp.463-5.
[31] October 1, 1899, n. 1

for our nation, so harshly hit by the barbaric acts committed in Louisiana."[32]

Predictably, the mission of the special agent sent by the federal government did not yield any results. The State Department chose the usual pseudo-solution of conceding an indemnity to the victims' families, despite the fact that the Italian embassy had not made any request of this kind. Ambassador Fava received unconditional support from Minister Emilio Visconti Venosta for his work on this case and for the persistence in demanding punishment for the perpetrators. He was praised by the minister for correctly representing "the thought of the Royal Government."[33] In practical terms, however, there had been no progress. In explaining the reasons for his pessimism, Fava estimated that the chance of a dignified solution was practically nil: "Our press is a little too optimistic in attributing to our initiatives [...] an effectiveness that in reality is not there."[34]

4. The Embassy Reacts

In reality, the pressure applied by the Italian embassy on President McKinley pushing him to "provide for the safety of foreigners with federal legislative initiatives" at the beginning raised hopes that some concrete result could be achieved. The presidential message of December 5, 1899, for the opening of the Fifty-Sixth Congress was received by Fava with overt satisfaction. President McKinley, in fact, dealt specifically with the lynching in Tallulah which, for the fourth time in a decade, had caused a conflict with the Italian government on the same issue. As Fava had long suggested, he proposed that "the local magistrates should lose jurisdiction over crimes committed in the states that violated the obliga-

---

[32] "Pei linciati di Tallulah l'ingerenza del Governo Federale." *La Tribuna* October 2, 1899.

[33] ASDMAE, idem. From MAE to the Italian Embassy in Washington, October 18, 1899.

[34] ASDMAE, idem. From the Italian Embassy in Washington to MAE, October 18, 1899.

tions undersigned by the federal government.[35] Legislative work had begun in both branches of Parliament in the attempt of finding a political and institutional solution that would be satisfactory to both countries."[36]

In the meantime Giuseppe Delfina, the brother-in-law of one of the lynching victims, who had to flee the area after being threatened, contacted the embassy in order to submit through diplomatic channels a request for indemnification for the damage he suffered when he had to abandon his home and all his possessions. Ambassador Fava, however, used his diplomatic skills to pursue a step-by-step strategy with a different timetable. He considered the request premature "because it could compromise my position of rejecting any offer of indemnification for the victims." Congress in fact was debating issues that were far more important, namely two bills on the juridical position of foreigners. Since Congress's default position was to award a compensation in any case, it was not tactically expedient to undermine the much tougher request by the Italian government that had caused the congressional debate of a much deeper principle. The indemnification would eventually be awarded anyway. "It is untimely to introduce a request related to the lynching that could be interpreted as the sign of willingness by the Royal Government to resolve the contention with the simple acceptance of a pecuniary compensation to the victims' families."[37]

The stakes were too high on the legislative level and the game had to be played with great skill: "In order for the two bills (Davis and Hitt) to be adopted in their entirety, it is crucial that Congress is not aware of

---

[35] ASDMAE, idem. From the Italian Embassy in Washington to MAE, December 5, 1899. Attached: Presidential address of December 5, 1899. See also FRUS 1900, pp. XXII-XXIII.

[36] See the bills offered by Congressman Hitt, attached to the report sent by the Embassy of Italy in Washington to MAE, January 12, 1900, in ASDMAE, ibidem.

[37] ASDMAE, ibidem. From the Italian Embassy in Washington to MAE, January 14, 1900.

even the slightest hint of a possible indemnity as a solution, not even if the initiative was started at the federal level."[38]

Unlike Fava, the Italian government had a more flexible position and nudged the ambassador to operate, through confidential channels, with the goal of obtaining some form of reparation at least for the victims' families, treating the Delfina issue as a separate case. "The ministry of Foreign Affairs," — Fava wrote, — "recommends that we inform privately and confidentially our counterparts that if the American government offered an indemnity to the Tallulah victims' families, the Royal Government would not consider itself authorized to deprive them of such benefit." The ambassador maintained instead that it was better to wait before putting forth the position of the Italian government, in consideration of the fact that the parliamentary situation of the Davis and Hitt bill had improved."

As a matter of fact, the situation for the American government was rather embarrassing. Secretary of State Hay refused to communicate to Fava the results of the investigation conducted by the special agent that had been sent by the federal government: "He said that revealing the findings would make him ashamed for his country." The indecent response by the governor of Louisiana, in turn, made Fava describe as "disgusting" the conduct of the Louisiana justice system. According to the ambassador, the indemnity was too easy a solution and a no-brainer for the federal government, given the difficulty or impossibility [...] to find different ways out: "The federal government is always willing to arrive at this solution, most of all if we hint that we would accept it."

The ambassador then went on to argue the correctness of his approach in this case, whose outcome, in his opinion, had gone farther than the simple reparation: "Whereas our diplomatic action in the Tallulah lynching has taken a different approach than the course we had followed in similar previous cases, we were able to influence the public opinion, the opinion of the President and, to an extent, the opinion of Congress, arguing that the necessity exists to provide adequate legislative

---

[38] ASDMAE, idem. From the Italian Embassy in Washington to MAE, January 20, 1900.

means for the security and protection of foreigners as prescribed by treaties." Fava's proposal was to put aside temporarily the issue of pecuniary reparation: "We should concern ourselves with avoiding any interference in the normal process of such a highly important legislative initiative, using parallel actions of a different nature such as the proposal of reparation [...] because, as in the past, the indemnification would be considered sufficient reparation by the American government and Congress and by everyone else."[39]

The political campaign for the presidential election of November 1900 paralyzed the work of Congress with regard to possible constitutional reforms.[40] President McKinley in June 1900 suggested that Congress, to be reconvened in the following month of December, should take on the request for reparation for the Tallulah victims. Ambassador Fava anticipated that the case would once again end with monetary compensation. He then proposed that the reparation be rejected on the basis of national dignity, knowing full well that the Italian government had a different view. "I am not in favor of accepting the indemnification and I believe that by rejecting it we would give a lesson to the Americans and defend our dignity. As to the indemnification to the families, we could take care of it ourselves."[41] In a report sent to the Ministry of Foreign Affairs the same day, Fava added solid arguments to his thesis, insisting that "by paying an indemnification, the Government and Congress, not to speak of the American public opinion, would conclude that it would be totally superfluous to add new legislation for the protection of foreigners, whose lives can be redeemed for a few dollars. [...] A pecuniary reparation would be allocated by Congress, as in the past, as an act of generosity and philanthropy but it would not close the contention. We need measures that in the future can guarantee the safety of our co-nationals." In case the Italian government decided otherwise, Fava indicated that he would defer to its decision. However, he stressed the consequences that could derive from accepting the indemnity, among which

---

[39] ASDMAE, idem. From the Italian Embassy in Washington to MAE, April 20, 1900.
[40] ASDMAE, idem. From the Italian Embassy in Washington to MAE, May 14, 1900.
[41] ASDMAE, idem. From the Italian Embassy in Washington to MAE, July 9, 1900.

would be a setback for the diplomatic contention between the two states: "In view of the presumable acceptance of a reparation, I am asking Your Excellency [the minister] to grant me permission to decline any responsibility in the case Congress resolves not to pursue the bill for the protection of foreigners that, with enormous effort, I was able to have brought to the floor."[42]

Minister Visconti Venosta was trying to find a way to mediate between the rightful rigor of Ambassador Fava and the fear that, in the end, the constitutional reform would not pass and the reparation would not be paid, leaving the Italian government with this burden. The Italian minister, therefore, proposed a compromise to solve the problem: delay the request for compensation until after the parliamentary debate on the constitutional reform. In a telegram to Ambassador Fava he wrote: "I recognize the unpleasant situation we would have to face if we obtained neither the legislative reform nor the indemnification. In this case we would be burdened with the responsibility to pay for every future case of this kind. It seems to me that your proposal can be supported, adding to it that the bill allowing the reparation should be presented only after Congress reintroduces the bill regarding the reform of federal jurisdiction."[43]

With the impending return of Congress from recess, and following the minister's directives, Fava resumed his pressure in favor of a constitutional reform. He sent a "personal and confidential note" to Secretary of State Hay, asking him "as a friendly gesture" to pass it on to President McKinley, hoping he would pressure Congress to take up the Davis and Hitt legislation. The ambassador also asked the president to express his condolences for the assassination of King Umberto, stressing that "your sympathetic message about the immense tragedy that struck the Italian people in the person of its beloved and bemoaned sovereign, would re-

---

[42] ASDMAE, idem. From the Italian Embassy in Washington to MAE, July 9, 1900.
[43] ASDMAE, idem. From the Italian Embassy in Washington to MAE, July 28, 1900.

verberate deeply in Italy" and would reconfirm his respect for the friendly nation.[44]

The developments seem to support the ambassador's view who was clearly satisfied at what seemed a real chance for an imminent constitutional revision. Moreover, President McKinley in his message, besides commemorating King Umberto, "remarked that the lynchers were still unpunished and that Italy, discarding from the beginning any possibility of indemnity, had reclaimed the strict application of principles of justice by virtue of international treaties. The President urged Congress to pass the Davis and Hitt legislation with the goal of transferring to the federal courts the jurisdiction of international cases of this nature where the responsibility of the federal government is involved." Greatly relevant was the fact that the president stressed the need to fill a constitutional vacuum: "It is a duty for us to remediate the constitutional vacuum that has brought and could further bring to such deadly results."

It was improbable that the effects of the two bills could be extended retroactively to the Tallulah incident. For that event the president recommended that Congress take care of the victims' families by means of an indemnity in the same amount as had been done in the past. Fava was clearly satisfied since "the President received positively our suggestions. He presented to Congress a request for indemnification not as a reparation requested by us for the lives of our co-nationals, but as a spontaneous act and demonstration of goodwill by this government." Just as important were the president's words about the lynchings. Although he had previously expressed his opinion on this matter, this time his statements were even more important in that they could be interpreted as direct pressure on Congress to approve the bills. "Lynching cannot be tolerated in a great civilized country like the United States: the courts, not the mobs, must enforce the penalties established by our laws."[45]

---

[44] ASDMAE, idem. From the Italian Embassy in Washington to MAE, November 26, 1900.
[45] ASDMAE, idem. From the Italian Embassy in Washington to MAE, December 3, 1900.

The truth was that, by asking for the standard indemnity of $2,000 for each victim, the president was only proposing that Congress compensate the victims with Italian citizenship, Giuseppe Difatta and Giovanni Cerami, with the usual motivation that deflected the issue of accountability, "without reference to the question of the United States' responsibility." Indeed, the reference by analogy was the response to the Walsenburg lynching of 1895. Only two of the victims received reparation, despite the effort by Fava with the secretary of state to extend the reparation also to the naturalized-American relatives of non-American victims. The secretary of state responded explaining that, in practical terms, he did not submit this specific request to Congress because it would certainly be rejected as a dangerous precedent that was not contemplated by the law and that would open the floodgate to every similar case involving non-naturalized families of American citizens. Secretary Hay, as partial compensation, gave the assurance that he would submit to Congress a request for reparation for Delfina who was forced to abandon his properties and belongings under threat of lynching.[46]

Congress approved the standard amount of $2,000 for each victim. The Italian minister had some reservations about this outcome. He expected that the victims would be compensated with an amount far larger that the $2,000 awarded to Delfina. Ambassador Fava responded that it would have been impossible to go over that limit: the Italians lynched in Walsenburg and in Hahnville, in addition to a Mexican citizen just recently victim of a similar act, had all received only $2,000 each.[47]

5. Erwin, Mississippi, 1901

Two Sicilians from Cefalù, Giovanni Serio and his son Vincenzo, were lynched in Erwin on July 11, 1901. They were door-to-door fruit and vegetable sellers. They were killed by rifle shots while they were sleeping outdoors on the roof of a house owned by a friend, Francesco

---

[46] ASDMAE, idem. From the Italian Embassy in Washington to MAE, February 5, 1901.
[47] ASDMAE, idem. From the Italian Embassy in Washington to MAE, May 10, 1901.

Cascio. A third person, Salvatore Liberto, who was also working with the Serios was also wounded. Cascio managed to escape and reported the massacre. The three casualties were still Italian citizens. The assassination of the two Italians and the wounding of the third were not the result of a violent confrontation, or the outcome of some long-standing dispute that could represent a potential danger for them. In fact they were sleeping outdoors without any reason to suspect an ambush. The only conflict they had been involved in had taken place months earlier for rather futile reasons. The Italian Consul in New Orleans, Natale Piazza, sent an agent, Tirelli [probably Adelelmo Luigi Tirelli] to investigate the facts and report back to him. Tirelli's reconstruction was based on the information he was able to gather from other Italians in the area. Eight months earlier the Serios lived in Glen Allen, near Erwin, where they ran a respectably successful business. A horse they owned often trespassed into the land owned by a certain G.B. Allen, owner of a large plantation. In several occasions Allen confiscated the animal protesting that it damaged his pasture and requesting the payment of one dollar as ransom for returning it. In one occasion Allen threatened at gunpoint one of the Serios who was complaining against this act of bullying. The next time the horse was confiscated, the older Serio, carrying rifle for self defense purposes, went directly to Allen's house to get back his horse. The same evening Allen and a group of other people went to the Serios house with the intent to kill them. The brother had been warned just in time and managed to flee to Greenville after being chased by an armed posse for six or seven miles.

In Greenville the Serios tried to restart the fruit-selling business but they weren't doing well. Their friend Francesco Cascio suggested that they move to Erwin where they could stay as his guests. They were reasonably reassured that Allen would not try to kill them again. Glen Allen was over six miles from Erwin and, in any case, the quarrel seemed to have cooled off. Tirelli's investigation also included the testimony of Rosario Liberto, seventeen years old, brother of the person who was wounded in the attack. The evening when the lynching took place, as he was about to leave Glen Allen where he worked to return home to Erwin, he ran into the town's doctor, Dr. Hollow, who warned him not to go back to Erwin because there was a plan to kill the Italians living in that village. The boy, terrified, told two *paesani*, Vincenzo Giglio and Giuseppe Butera who ran to the town's telephone office, to urge the other Italians in Erwin to flee and find safety elsewhere. At the office they were told that the telephone was out of order. Unconvinced, they kept insisting they needed to make an urgent call. The employee replied that it wasn't their business to spread the news to people in Erwin and threw them out. At this point the two Italians, afraid they would be assassinated, avoided reporting the information to the sheriff. When they spoke to Tirelli they stated that they were willing to testify in court under oath. This was additional overwhelming evidence about the conspiracy-complicity surrounding Allen's violent plan. Tirelli in a survey of the crime scene counted thirty-five bullet holes, which led him to conclude that several shooters were involved.[48]

The Italian-language press in the United States immediately denounced the events with heavy accusations against the "most civilized" American population and against the feebleness of the Italian government with loud demands for "strong and resolute action." The New York *Progresso Italo-Americano* commented on the devastation brought onto Italians by the news of yet another lynching.

"Once again American hands drip with Italian blood. Once again savage brutality triumphs at the expense of free citizens. Once again the spilled blood denounces the failure of the law and the shame of primitive practices. Lynch's Law is the name given to a crime that carries in itself the vestiges of barbarism — with a savage mob running amok and abandoning themselves to truculent acts: this is something that terrifies and causes horror."[49]

In the general tone of condemnation expressed by the entire Italian-language press in the United States, some nuanced differences emerged

---

[48] ASDMAE, Italian Diplomatic Delegation in Washington (1901-1909), b.1 47, f. 3225. From the Italian Consulate in New Orleans to the Italian Embassy in Washington, July 19, 1901.

[49] *Il Progresso Italo-Americano* July 13, 1901.

in the degree of revulsion. The New York Italian newspaper *L'Araldo*, for instance, in a comment about an article that appeared in *Il Progresso* criticized the fatalism of calling lynching "an endemic and incurable disease of this country," and the paradoxical comparison that an Italian who migrated to Brazil could fall victim to yellow fever while in the United States he could be lynched.[50]

6. THE EMBASSY REACTS

The usual procedure was started, like in previous cases of lynching. First came the protest by Italian *chargé d'affaires* in Washington Carignani to his counterpart at the State Department[51] who responded with the traditional formula of regret for the tragedy and the promise that everything will be done to find and punish the offenders. "He expressed the regret of the government for the recent lynching of two Italians in Mississippi and indicated that every effort was being made to identify and bring the culprits to justice."[52] The Italian government's protest was immediately interpreted by a part of the American press as the usual ruse to obtain monetary reparation, as in previous recent situations. According to the *Daily Progress* of July 22, for instance: "The Italian protest was undoubtedly mounted with the perspective of the kind of certain indemnity similar to what the Italian government easily obtained in the lynching cases of New Orleans and Tallulah."[53]

And once again the investigation ordered by the governor of Mississippi, exactly like in previous cases, showed that the local authorities had not made any effort to identify the authors of the crime.[54] Not particularly surprised at the outcome, *chargé d'affaires* Carignani wrote to the person in charge at the State Department complaining that "several days

---

[50] *L'Araldo* July 25, 1901.
[51] ASDMAE, idem. From the Italian Embassy in Washington to MAE, July 24, 1901.
[52] *The Washington Post* July 22, 1901.
[53] "Italian Government," *Daily Progress* July 22, 1901.
[54] This is made even more obvious by the meager reward for the capture of the lynchers: $100 from the governor's office and $100 from the County. See FRUS 1901, p. 289.

after the crime, it doesn't seem that a judiciary inquiry has been started, which is the very first step for the prosecution of a crime." It was obvious that the criminals could rely on a network of accomplices, first and foremost the person in charge of the telephone office. "We have full confirmation of the depositions by Vincenzo Giglio and Giuseppe Butera in which they declare that the day before the lynching took place they tried to alert Vincenzo Serio about the lynching plans, but they were denied the use of the telephone three times. The embassy also requested protection for the witnesses, after noticing the existence of an atmosphere of fear and intimidation surrounding the Italians living in that village. "It is of capital importance that protection be provided to the witnesses so as to insure that they will be able to testify freely. Strong intimidation is in place, as we can attest by the obstacles that our agents encountered in their investigations. Even the wounded victim claims he knows nothing or close to nothing."[55]

The American press tried to deny that this act of violence fell under the rubric of a lynching, arguing that the classic modalities of lynching were not present since the victims had not been taken from a prison. Notwithstanding the many variables present in different lynchings, the press insisted on the differences, in particular the premeditation factor. The episode was ascribed to the category of bloody actions. Acting Consul in New Orleans Papini, however, wrote to the embassy presenting a very different thesis based on strong arguments: "That this was a lynching is also proved by the warning given by Doctor Hollow (or Hanna) of Glen Allen to the youngster Liberto, brother of the wounded victim Salvatore Liberto, alerting him of what was going to happen to Vincenzo Serio. Other proof is the refusal by the telephone operator of Glen Allen to let V. Giglio use the telephone to urge the Serios to flee. We also know that a telephone call was made to Glen Allen on the morning of July 9, with the information that Vincenzo Serio was on the train to Erwin. This latest circumstance was communicated by means of an anonymous letter, however, it does have value in that it explains the reason

---

[55] ASDMAE, idem. From the Italian Embassy in Washington to MAE, July 30, 1901.

why the telephone operator denied use of the telephone to the same V. Giglio." The message contained the usual accusations against the local and state authorities "whose goal is to drag things on so that eventually everything will be forgotten."[56]

Whether the Erwin episode was classified as a lynching was not simply a matter of semantic disputes. The classification was extremely important: if it was considered as a common crime, the victims' families would have no chance of obtaining reparation from the government. Not coincidentally, this was the thesis of both the American press and Acting Secretary of State David Hill. The embassy was determined to prove that the killings were a true lynching and was not willing to back down. Carignani wrote to Minister Prinetti that "the grand jury assembled by the sheriff stated that the victims' death was *God's will*, which is exactly the same formula used for lynchings."[57] Attached to the report to Minister Prinetti, Carignani also sent to Rome the definition of lynching according to the state of Ohio, which included any illegal act committed by a mob.[58] He further explained that "in general the laws of one state constitute a precedent for other states."

Minister Prinetti had given instructions for the hiring of a local private detective to look for the offenders but the embassy responded that "both private agencies and detectives of the secret police refused to take the job. This is in line with the traditions of the South where lynching is not considered a crime and where anyone trying to track down the assassins would be exposed to the danger of reprisals." The cultural factors

---

[56] ASDMAE, Serie Politica "P" (1891-1916), b. 680, f. 856. From the Italian Consulate in New Orleans to the Italian Embassy in Washington, attached to the report of August 1, 1901.

[57] ASDMAE, idem. From the Italian Embassy in Washington to MAE, August 3, 1901.

[58] "Lynching was defined by Ohio laws as follows: any group of individuals gathered for any illegal purpose, with the intention of causing damage, wounds or offenses to anyone, claiming the exercise of correctional power on other people by means of violence and without the authority of the law, for such purpose will be considered a mob and every act of violence perpetrated by it against another person will constitute lynching." 92 Ohio Laws, 136, in ASDMAE, idem.

were to be added to the low level of professionalism in the investigation: "Police officers and private investigators in the southern states generally are not considered very capable, to the point that Americans themselves do not hire them." Ambassador Carignani then tried to convince the federal government to send its secret police, offering that the Italian government would foot the bill: "This would demonstrate how deep our interest is in finding the culprits and would also reassure us as to the effectiveness of the investigation."[59] The federal government, however, was convinced that the local authorities were finally actively working to find the offenders and rejected the request explaining that "there would be no reason to send agents of the central government." This reassurance led Carignani to believe, at least temporarily, that "the Mississippi authorities [were] demonstrating more zeal."[60]

Minister Prinetti was less optimistic and became critical of the trust Carignani had placed in the activities of the governor of Mississippi and of the federal government: "Unfortunately [...] so far there is no evidence that your impression is about to be translated into concrete and effective action." In reality no honorable solution was appearing on the horizon. All pointed the opposite direction, starting with the statements by the jury convened by the county sheriff that the authors of the crime were unknown; continuing with the ineptitude of the state's governor; and finishing with the federal government's refusal to take action, barricaded behind the limits imposed by the Constitution, "to the point of rejecting the suggestion to use at our expense the secret police, whose members — we presume — are less susceptible to local pressures." Prinetti added: "The inertia is so patent and willful that we can not rest and avoid pointing to the federal Government."

The minister also underlined a new aspect that made this case even more egregious than the previous ones: the Italian victims had not been

---

[59] ASDMAE, Italian Diplomatic Delegation in Washington (1901-1909), b.1 47, f. 3225. From the Italian Consulate in New Orleans to the Italian Embassy in Washington, August 14, 1901.

[60] ASDMAE, Serie Politica "P" (1891-1916), b. 680, f. 856. From the Italian Embassy in Washington to MAE, August 21, 1896.

charged with any offense: "This case even lacks the circumstances that in other situations were used as an excuse for a lynching, namely that it was an act of popular justice that replaced the function of the magistrates but that was exercised against people who were guilty, or confessed their guilt — or where at least the crowd was convinced of their guilt. Whatever we want to call this, whether lynching or any other name, this is a brutal assassination caused by petty motives against people who had not been even suspected or indicted in any judiciary inquiry." Prinetti drew very pessimistic conclusions although he was not yet willing to give up completely. "It is too repugnant for me to think that the government and the people of this glorious Republic may go along with something that would be the negation of any form of civilized justice."[61]

The pessimism of the minister turned out to be right about the posture of federal and state institutions and also about the climate of intimidation against the witnesses. In a report to the consulate's Natale Piazza, Agent Tirelli talked about the reticence and terror that dominated among the local Italians "all full of fear and regret for the statements they made." In particular the main witness, Salvatore Liberto, who had been wounded, was convinced that his testimony would mean certain death. At first Liberto had promised Papini that he would appear in court and render the same deposition. Later, however, "he refused to appear in court, explaining that if he talked in front of the jury, that would be the end of his life: in time he would be killed like a dog by the mob of Washington County where he earns his living." The other Italians in the area were afraid of ending up the same way: "Everybody is fixated on this idea, and in fact as soon as they found out that I was in the area they managed to disappear."[62] After reassuring them, Tirelli was able to convince them to go to court and testify.

---

[61] ASDMAE, Italian Diplomatic Delegation in Washington (1901-1909), b.1 47, f. 3225. From MAE to the Italian Embassy in Washington, August 22, 1901.
[62] ASDMAE, Serie Politica "P" (1891-1916), b. 680, f. 856. From the Italian Consulate in New Orleans to the Italian Embassy in Washington, August 14, 1896. Attached to the report from the Italian Embassy in Washington to MAE, September 22, 1901.

The grand jury met on September 13, 1901, to evaluate if enough evidence was available to proceed to an indictment. The verdict was negative to the great consternation of the Italian government. According to Acting Consul Papini, there could be two possible explanations: "Either the depositions made at the consulate were not *repeated identically* at the hearing [...], or the prosecutor has discarded the depositions in order to save the town's honor and good reputation." His sad conclusions left no hope: "Regardless of the reason, we can legitimately conclude that any future attempt to obtain justice would end up in failure." Papini, then, proposed to focus on at least obtaining reparation for the surviving relatives. The way to obtain it would be to sue the telephone company whose employee didn't allow the use of the means that could have warned the victims and could have prevented the lynching. Papini believed there was enough evidence to indict the person who had denied the use of the phone. Incidentally, this person was the brother of one of the lynchers.[63]

Minister Prinetti reacted with dismay and disbelief and with increased worry about the government's future ability to provide protection to Italians. "Such disgraceful neglect and inertia are reassuring the authors of these acts. In the future this will have the effect of encouraging more massacres whose victims, unfortunately, will again be our fellow citizens."

At this point the controversy no longer involved only the state of Mississippi but was raised to the level of diplomatic relations between the two governments. "In such a state, I see the need to protest with the Federal Government for this process whose outcome is a true and full denial of justice." Prinetti gave instructions to Carignani to draft a formal protest to be approved by the minister himself before sending it over to State Department.[64] *Chargé d'affaires* Carignani placed the episodes of discrimination against Italians within the general atmosphere that was getting progressively more dangerous for them. Writing to Minister Pri-

---

[63] ASDMAE, idem. September 16, 1896.
[64] ASDMAE, Italian Diplomatic Delegation in Washington (1901-1909), b.1 47, f. 3225. From MAE to the Italian Embassy in Washington, October 10, 1901.

netti he stated: "The acts of violence and armed aggressions against Italians have increased while the protection afforded to them by the authorities is lagging. We must lament in the last three months the occurrence of several crimes of this kind, which are proof that my claims are correct."

The *chargé d'affaires* suggested to Minister Prinetti that the formal protest to the government of the United States for the violation of the treaty concerning the protection of the respective citizens also included the threat or determination that Italy would consider itself relieved of the obligations contained in the treaty. "I have been instructed to relay that since the Government of the United States --- because of its current legislation -- once again has failed to protect effectively the lives and properties of Italian citizens, the Royal Government is considering whether it should resolve that it is now relieved in front of the American citizens in this Kingdom of the obligations stipulated in Article 3 of the treaty of February 26, 1871." In his letter to Prinetti, Carignani added: "I made sure to remark that Article 3 of our Civil Code includes the liberal principle that foreigners are accorded the full enjoyment of civil rights even in the absence of a reciprocity clause. This makes the statement about our intentions even stronger."[65]

As the chances of capturing the culprits became more and more feeble, the Italian authorities were forced to acknowledge the umpteenth failure. Minister Prinetti recognized that his initial hopes were an illusion: "I was wrong when in one of my letters I was still expressing hope that the dastardly crime would not go unpunished." In the end the only realistic option left was to send the usual formal protest note to the American government. "The Royal government of Italy has lost all confidence in the local authority and in particular in the magistrates. We would fail in our duty if we didn't formally protest for the violation of the treaty and the flagrant denial of justice." The hope for a future modification of the Constitution was still standing. "I hope our action will have the effect of hastening a reform in your jurisdiction which has been

---

[65] ASDMAE, idem. From the Italian Embassy in Washington to MAE, October 10, 1901.

solemnly recommended in a presidential message and promised many times, but that so far has remained at the state of proposal."[66] The new ambassador, Edmondo Mayor de Planches, reported back to the minister the content of the answer by Undersecretary of State Hill, who expressed his personal regret for the events and recognized the need of reparation.[67]

7. THE ECHO IN ITALY

In the Italian Senate the new episode of violence against Italian emigrants started a heated debate with an attack against the government of the United States. Former Ambassador to the United States Fava, appointed to the Senate in 1901, in the session of December 20 submitted a hard-hitting question to Minister Prinetti on the on-going dispute and on the intentions of the ministry. At first he attacked vehemently the verdict of the grand jury of September 13, 1901, that contained the motivation of "lack of sufficient evidence" against any person responsible for the lynching which, incidentally, was labeled as "God's will." Fava commented about a ritual that was becoming ever more grotesque: "The verdict is totally identical in substance to those emitted in four previous lynchings. The conduct of the American government in the previous three cases was also identical." He repeated that the limits imposed by the Constitution only allowed the federal government to urge the various governors to abide by international treaties, limiting its action to exhortations to find and punish the culprits. The former ambassador also recognized that things didn't go much differently when the State Department sent an agent from the Justice Department to conduct an independent investigation, as in the case of the Tallulah lynching in

---

[66] ASDMAE, Serie Politica "P" (1891-1916), b. 680, f. 856. From MAE to the Italian Embassy in Washington, October 28, 1901. The rest of the formal protest, dated November 14, 1901, in FRUS, pp. 297-8.
[67] ASDMAE, idem. From the Italian Embassy in Washington to MAE, November 16, 1901.

1899. "This separate inquiry also gave no fruit because of the ill will of the local state authorities who did not assist the investigator in the least."

Fava credited himself and former Minister Visconti Venosta with reacting harshly to the impunity given to the Tallulah killers, implicitly criticizing the acquiescence of current Minister Prinetti. "Our honor prevented us from tolerating such a state of things. Under the enlightened leadership and great competence of a statesman of great value like the Hon. Visconti Venosta, our major concern was to force the Federal Government to establish its exclusive jurisdiction in the case of lynching of foreigners."

Credit for pushing the president of the United States to propose to Congress the two constitutional reform bills on the relations between the federal government and the states went to the hard work coordinated by the former ambassador and the former minister. "President McKinley understood the merit of our demands: the outcome of long negotiations with him was in two messages delivered to Congress in 1899 and 1900 urging Congress to assign to the Federal Courts full jurisdiction in international cases of this nature. With memorable words he stated that 'in these cases *at the very end* the federal government is accountable, and has the responsibility to remediate the constitutional omission that has led and could lead again to deplorable consequences.'"

President McKinley's support for constitutional reform led to the introduction in Congress of two identical bills by Davis and Hitt stipulating that an act of violence committed in a state or territory of the United States that violated the rights of a foreign citizen — under the provisions of an international treaty between the two states — would be regarded as a crime according to the local laws but also as a crime against the peace and dignity of the United States, and would therefore be pursued in a similar way and with similar penalties by the courts of the states involved, subject to the local statutes of limitation, and adjudicated in Federal Court. In the case of a guilty verdict, the sentence would be carried out according to the provisions established for crimes committed under federal law.

The Senate Judiciary Committee approved the bill unanimously. However, the bill didn't reach the floor in time before Congress adjourned. On September 15, 1901, President McKinley was assassinated. He was the first and only president to show any sensibility for these problems. With his death the prospect for the two bills began to fade. His successor, Theodore Roosevelt, was much more responsive to the arguments of southern states that had always been hostile to any interference by the federal government in internal questions. Senator Fava was fully aware of the political shift and predicted, with great disappointment, that the constitutional reform bills would be abandoned. "I was really surprised that President Roosevelt, in his recent message, did not even mention the legislative reforms dear to his predecessor's heart that would have led to a dignified and just legal solution of this thorny contention. Moreover, we have not heard of any initiative by Congress about the transfer of prosecution of lynchings to the federal courts."

Senator Fava's parliamentary question to Minister Prinetti aimed to put the minister "into the corner," asking if he would pursue the same policy as that of his precedessor Visconti Venosta; and if he hoped to ensure that new bills, similar to those that had expired, would be introduced to the new Congress. With a hint of irony, Fava also asked the minister if had found "a new, more effective way, to reach the goal we all aim for." With regard to the likely offer of indemnity by the federal government to the victims' families, Fava reminded the assembly that after the Tallulah lynching of 1899, the indemnification was spontaneously offered to the Italian government: "It would have been wiser to reject it, for reasons I will explain later." The senator urged his colleagues to notice that "Congress awards these indemnities only as an act of generous help to the surviving family members. By giving alms, Americans believe they have paid their debt. The rejection of this blood price would have been much more effective in that it would have shocked the American public opinion." The majority of the Senate agreed with Senator Fava and his proposal to reject the reparation likely to be offered by the American government. "The Italian public opinion, better informed about the frequency of these atrocities, will understand that it is in the interest of our dignity to reject reparation from the United States, in case they should offer it. We prefer that every means necessary be used to obtain from the Washington government exemplary justice and the legislative measures necessary to ensure that Italians resident in the United States receive the protection to which they are entitled by virtue of the treaties."

Minister Prinetti responded to Senator Fava defending the action of the government, promising that he would continue to provide the Italian citizens in the United States with a form of protection that would not be "too cocky," since in general Italians were well accepted. "The government, even in this sad circumstance, has fulfilled its duty. The Italian diplomatic functionaries cannot be accused of lack of trying or insufficient diligence. It is not their fault if even in this case the results were not what we would have liked to see and get." The minister agreed with Fava that "the indemnity cannot be considered as reparation for the crime committed." He promised that he would not request it, however; he didn't think it would be right for the Italian government to force the victims' relatives to renounce a reparation offered spontaneously, in that this was in the interest of the third party. Prinetti, therefore, would not request an indemnity as "blood price" for Italian citizens, but would not oppose an indemnity offered to the victims' relatives.[68]

8. THE ECHO IN THE UNITED STATES

The Italian position was supported by a part of the American public opinion. With the exception of the southern states, a consensus was emerging on the need for a constitutional reform. The *New York Tribune*, for instance, wrote that "more needs to be done than pay reparation for the victims or their surviving relatives." The newspaper acknowledged the patience of the Italian government on this issue, arguing that the conduct of the American government was more becoming to a country like Turkey than to the United States: "The Italian government showed a lot of patience but there is a limit to the gracious toleration for

---

[68] AP, Senato del Regno, Legislatura XXI, Discussioni, Tornata December 20, 1901.

a situation that we would expect from Turkey, with its genius for diplomatic irresponsibility, and not from the United States."

The newspaper criticized the ineptitude of the government and Congress, which had justified their lack of political will with the excuse of the constitutional vacuum. "The lack of power on the part of federal authorities today is not due to our Constitution but simply to the negligence of our legislators in the use of their power. The Constitution gives to the central government full power in all the cases related to treaties. However, Congress never took action to assign to the federal courts the jurisdiction over cases based on the violation of the treaties on the rights of foreigners."[69] A second newspaper, *The Evening Star*, remarked that the contention between the two nations once again could not be solved only by means of a simple indemnification to the families of the victims. "The Italian government is not looking for blood money. Asking for monetary compensation would correspond to putting a price on a cadaver. It would be like calculating in dollars and cents the price of an Italian's blood." Any reparation would at most concern the victims' families, not the Italian government: "Such indemnities are for the offended people, not for the Italian government whose judgment is that the issue is much more important than the individual compensation given to individuals."[70]

One year later, in the imminence of the State of the Union Address to Congress on December 15, 1902, Ambassador Mayor de Planches wrote to Minister Prinetti to inform him that he had contacted the secretary of state to remind him that the Italian government counted on a spontaneous initiative by the government and Congress to offer reparation — in whatever form they chose, "for the consequences of the lack of protection" guaranteed by the treaty, with the provision that "this Embassy will not be a party" to the decision.[71]

---

[69] "Italy's Just Complaint." *New York Tribune* December 27, 1901.
[70] "Italy's Contention." *The Evening Star* December 25, 1901.
[71] ASDMAE, idem. From the Italian Embassy in Washington to MAE, December 6, 1902.

Two days after the inauguration of Congress, on December 13, Secretary of State John Hay briefed President Roosevelt on the Erwin episode with a note in which he discussed the request for compensation without any word of condemnation for the conduct of local authorities, nor about any responsibility, and no mention whatsoever of the institutional conflict between individual states and the federal government over the lynching perpetrated "by means of an armed mob." "Despite the cordial cooperation of the federal government with the governor of the state to secure the culprits to justice, it seems all our efforts were in vain." Hay resolved to ask Congress to approve the indemnification, on the precedent of similar action after the lynchings in Walsenburg and Tallulah, under the guise of "a concession with no reference to the issue of responsibility by the United States," the exact same formula used in presidential messages in previous cases that contained the recommendation that Congress approved the compensation without acknowledging any responsibility.[72]

In March 1903, Congress approved the sum of $5,000.[73] The concession of an indemnification did not quiet the polemics in Italy, as reflected in a number of statements of politicians. The Hon. Cirmeni presented a parliamentary question on April 28, 1903, to Minister Prinetti about the diplomatic controversy recently concluded with the concession of an indemnification to the families of the Italians lynched in Erwin. Undersecretary of Foreign Affairs Baccelli replied on May 7, 1903, stating that two years after the strong protest by the Italian government to the American government, the issue could not be considered solved.[74]

The *New York Times*, reporting the discussion in the Italian parliament about the Erwing lynching, on May 7, 1903, observed that the Italian government had no role in the concession of the indemnification "as it could never accept a blood prize, although at the same time it can-

---

[72] "Killing of Italian Subjects at Erwin, Miss." Message from the President of the United States, Senate, 57th Congress, 2nd session, Document No. 40, December 15, 1902.

[73] ASDMAE, idem. From the Italian Embassy in Washington to MAE, March 7, 1903.

[74] AP, Camera dei Deputati, Discussioni, vol. 8, Tornata April 28, 1903, p. 7061, and tornata May 7, 1903, pp. 7306-7.

not force the offended parties to reject the indemnification." The newspaper clearly explained the reason why the two constitutional reform bills had not been passed by Congress: "The individual states are jealous of their autonomy."[75] Undersecretary Baccelli also mentioned a rather questionable "quantitative" thesis to explain the failure of Congress to pass a constitutional reform. In his view, the states rejected federal jurisdiction because the number of foreign citizens lynched was too small compared to that of American citizens: "For every European citizen lynched, every year there are 150 lynchings of American citizens. It is rather difficult, in this situation, to apply pressure to change American legislation."[76]

In his reply to Undersecretary Baccelli, the Hon. Cirmeni complained that the compensation was too low and quoted an acerbic cartoon that appeared in an Italian newspaper published in the United States, depicting the American secretary of state handing a purse to the Italian ambassador saying: "These Italians are so cheap that it may be worth it to lynch them all."[77]

Undersecretary Baccelli also declared that one of the reasons why the culprits had not been identified was the reluctance of Italian witnesses to testify. Cirmeni rebuked and defended the Italians, justifying their fear of being deposed in a climate of "Italian hunting": "If those witnessed had testified, we would have had other lynchings. The witnesses would have been slaughtered under the very eyes of local authorities."[78]

The Italian newspaper *L'Araldo*, published in New York, was extremely critical of the Italian government. On May 8, 1903, in a comment on the parliamentary debate on the Erwin lynching stated that the victims "from their tombs demand vengeance and cry for shame to fall

---

[75] "Italian Views of the Lynchings in America" *The New York Times* May 8, 1903 (5).

[76] AP, Camera dei Deputati, Legislatura XXI, Discussioni, Tornata May 7, 1903. The minutes of the session mentions an ironic comment to the statements by Baccelli. "A voice from the far left shouted: 'Free Lynching in a Free State."

[77] Ibidem. The minutes of the session reported the comment of the "voice" of a member, obviously poorly informed, who claimed: "They pay more for blacks."

[78] Ibidem.

on the cowardly and the pavid." In an article under the headline "Erwineide," the paper shouted: "Twenty-two brave months later, in our Parliament someone just woke up thinking that the Erwin incident isn't over yet! On this side of the Atlantic, instead, the Treasury Department of the North American Union is already in possession of a receipt, signed by the ambassador of the king of Italy, in exchange for the sum of $5,000, the blood price, accepted on behalf of the families of Serio and Liberto." The newspaper attacked with harsh tones the acquiescence of the Italian government and commented with deep disappointment on the applause given by the Italian Chamber of Deputies to Undersecretary Baccelli in his response to the Hon. Cirmeni. Just as harshly *L'Araldo* denounced the amount of money awarded to the victims' families, a sum that was considered miserable. The criticism focused on the "infamy of accepting the insulting charity of $5,000, equal to 25,000 Lira, for the lives of three fellow citizens, whereas American courts award compensations of $30,000, or $50,000 or $100,000 to unfortunates killed in a train wreck or by an accidental explosion — not premeditated murders like lynchings." The fact that the indemnity was not paid directly by the American consular authority in Italy but through an official representative of the Italian government in the United States made the conduct of the Italian government even more questionable and grievous. *L'Araldo* stressed the "naïveté of government officials and legislators about American affairs, and in particular about the relations with Italy for what pertains to the permanent and uncontrollable practice of lynching."

In the article there was no trace of optimism about possible future solutions: "We know that the American government will not give in to pressures from foreigners to modify the Constitution. We also know that the filthy savagery of the America people will not drop the enjoyment of killing Italians." The main target of the newspaper was Minister Prinetti: "The Italian Parliament had the duty to expel from the Chamber its member, Minister Prinetti who, on December 20, 1901, in order to silence the anger of Fava, confessed that he had to swallow the declaration from Washington that the lynching happened 'by the will of God,'" and that the government would certainly protect the immigrants, albeit "with not too much vigor!" The article continued with an exasperated and harsh tone accusing the ministry of committing a "state crime," and calling for the impeachment of the minister: "It would have been much more expedient, more effective and more respondent to the national spirit, if at the news of the State crime committed by the ministry in the indemnification affair, the Honorable Cirmeni had submitted a motion for the impeachment of the minister who imposed on the King's ambassador to negotiate the indemnification."[79]

The Erwin episode, like all the other lynchings of Italians, was closed with the usual "blood price" as compensation for the failure to identify and punish the culprits and without any guarantee of justice in the future. In this climate of discouragement and cynicism, Attorney Gino Speranza, corresponding secretary of the Society for the Protection of Italian Immigrants in New York —an association officially recognized by the Italian government— was appointed by the general commissary on emigration with the task of conducting an investigation on the maltreatment of Italian immigrants in West Virginia. The report drafted by Speranza in May 1903 was issued two weeks before an ambush that resulted in the killing of an Italian in Davis, West Virginia. In a passage of the report to the embassy, Speranza discussed the sad conclusion of the Erwin case and concluded in pessimistic tones: "I am sure that one of these days, when the facts I am describing are published, the government will ask if, after discovering the abuses, we did punish the offenders. For instance, I noticed the question by the Hon. Cirmeni on the Erwin episode and the reaction of the Chamber, stupefied that the culprits weren't punished. The reason for that, as far as I am concerned, is the same reason why there will be no punishment for the facts that I am currently investigating."

The reasons for the predictable impunity were, in Speranza's view, merely economical, namely the impossibility of affording the legal expense. "Here in West Virginia it would be impossible to win a law suit

---

[79] "Erwineide." *L'Araldo* May 8, 1903.

against the bosses unless one were able to afford the following costs." The attorney then listed the various items necessary: minimum $10,000 for the lawyers, expenses for finding witnesses, for detectives and for advertisements in the newspapers. "Maybe this summary table looks excessive, but I base my certainty on the facts and there is no other way to get a favorable sentence."[80] The conclusions by Ambassador Mayor were just as dejected: "We already knew all this, more or less, from other notorious events. But it is probably useful to repeat it to avoid any illusion about what can be obtained from the American system of justice and at what price.[81] The ambassador, however, failed to fully capture the substantial difference between the economic aspect discussed by Speranza and the eminently political aspect of the lynching of Italians that involved directly the two governments.

9. Ashdown, Arkansas, 1901

This case concerned the assassination, or the lynching, on August 1901, of an Italian, Giuseppe Buzzotta, from Castelvetrano. According to the reconstruction made by Papini, acting consul in New Orleans, he "was killed during a riot by American workers, supported by public law enforcement officers." Papini immediately asserted that it would be practically impossible to disprove the official version issued by the local authorities that blamed Bazzotta for provoking the incident. The problem was compounded by the difficulty to find witnesses willing to testify. Often the witnesses initially would declare themselves ready to testify but then, because of intimidation, recanted on their depositions or refused to appear in court: "Usually Italian witnesses are quick with wide and elaborate narrations when they speak with the representatives of the Italian Government, but later, either because they lack conscience, or due to intimidation or other pressures, when they are facing the grand

---

[80] The report by Speranza, dated May 15, 1903, was published in *Bollettino Emigrazione*, 1903, 14. The letter from Speranza to MAE is in ASDMAE, idem. From the Italian Embassy to Washington to MAE, May 20, 1903.
[81] ASDMAE, ibidem.

jury or in court with equal ease they change or deny the original depositions."[82]

One month after the episode, it was still impossible to obtain credible and definitive information. Ambassador Mayor wrote to Minister Prinetti: "We haven't been able to establish if [...] this was a common bloody crime or a true lynching, as some believe." The ambassador was planning to discuss with the secretary of state this case and also other "frequent bloody crimes, either lynchings or not, in which our fellow citizens are victims, without the kind of protection they are entitled to by the authorities, both by virtue of principles of humanity and by force of the treaties."[83]

In this case the formalities were followed. The assassin was duly prosecuted, the witnesses testified but the trial itself turned out to be a farce. The initial declarations by Italian witnesses were confirmed by some American newspapers that showed how this was a voluntary homicide. "The judge — Mayor wrote — instead decided this was involuntary homicide or without criminal intent."[84] The outcome left many questions open, among which was the fact that the Italian witnesses who could testify that the crime was committed voluntarily, either were not called to testify or gave statements that were different from those given in the preliminary depositions.

The Italian-language press in the United States once again erupted in indignation, placing this episode in the context of the competition for work among various ethnic groups. *La Tribuna* wrote: "We have new details on the depraved lynching of a poor Italian worker. A group of Italian workers is employed on the construction of the 'Kansas City Southern Railroad.' Here, just like in every other place, Italian workers are eagerly sought after because for the same salary they are much more productive than the ever-complaining drunkard Irish or lazy blacks."

---

[82] ASDMAE, Serie Politica "P" (1891-1916), b. 682, f. 871. From the Italian Consulate in New Orleans to MAE, October 15, 1901.

[83] ASDMAE, idem. From the Italian Embassy in Washington to MAE. November 25, 1901.

[84] ASDMAE, idem. From the Italian Embassy in Washington to MAE. April 29, 1902.

The newspaper reported the reconstruction of the events that "nailed" the responsibility of the murder on a group of about one hundred "indigenous" workers, armed with rifles, who had mercilessly terrorized and threatened harmless Italian workers and killed Buzzotta." *La Tribuna* lamented and denounced the lack of protection for Italian immigrants by the Italian government, mentioning as proof that even Erwin's lynchers had not been found. "The Italian colony is rightfully indignant and is still waiting for effective action by the Italian government. If nothing happens everyone will be persuaded that it is useless to spend money for ambassadors and embassies since all they are good at is acting like the diplomats of [...] the Grande Duchess of Gerolstein."[85] Just as stern was another comment published by the newspaper: "Once again this proves that in too many states of the Union there is a chronic and widespread habit of treating Italians worse than the ancient Helots, with no spirit of humanity and justice. How long will our flesh and our names be subjected to the offenses and scorn of such scum — protected and made even more cocky by total impunity?"[86]

10. Davis, West Virginia, 1903

This episode wasn't a true lynching. Rather, as Ambassador Mayor described, it was an attack against Italians with "some characteristics of a lynching." The event took place in the context of a labor conflict and competition for jobs among ethnic groups. The ambassador reported that on May 29, 1903, in Davis, West Virginia, during the night "a box full of dynamite exploded under a house where 37 of our fellow Italians were sleeping." The results were tragic: one person died immediately from the effects of the explosion and a second died a few days later from his injuries. From the fragments of news that could be gathered, it seemed that the bombing was caused by competition for jobs and was aiming at terrorizing the Italian workers and forcing them to abandon

---

[85] The reference is to the *opera buffa* by J. Offenbach *La Grande Duchesse de Gerolstein* (1867).
[86] "Gli Italiani in America." *La Tribuna* August 24, 1901.

the place. The Italian consul in Philadelphia moved quickly to contact the police superintendent in Davis, demanding the most vigorous protective measures for the local Italian population.[87] The investigation conducted by Speranza that we previously introduced, had revealed the existence of maltreatment of Italian workers in West Virginia.[88] The report described a terrifying picture of their living conditions, ranging from intimidation to "brutal terrorism." These included recruitment practices by Italian bosses with no scruples; the abuses by store owners who had the monopoly on the sale of every possible item in the encampments; and the impossibility of leaving the camp. "Those labor camps — Speranza wrote in his investigation-denunciation — look like deserts, livable only by feral animals. [...] The isolation makes the men anxious to run away. It is proven that armed guards are employed to intimidate workers and to prevent them from leaving the camp. As far as labor organizations are concerned, in West Virginia union members are more or less the same number as non-union workers: this creates a climate of conflicts and reprisals." Italian workers at Camp Davis at that time belonged to the non-union faction and were considered "scabs."

The murder, or lynching, was made possible by the neglect of public authorities "despite the fact that it had been predicted for a long time." This element enabled the victims' families to request an indemnification from the American government.

Giovanni Angelone submitted a request immediately to the Italian embassy to process his claim with the American government for $25,000 as reparation for the death of his brother Vincenzo, due to the lack of protection by local authorities.

Without much enthusiasm, the usual official steps were taken by the Italian consul in Philadelphia with the governor of the state and by the embassy with the secretary of state "to obtain, we hope, the punishment of the culprits." The embassy was rather pessimistic both about the chance of a trial and the chance of obtaining an indemnification: "About

---

[87] ASDMAE, idem. From the Italian Embassy in Washington to MAE. June 7, 1903.
[88] The report drafted by Speranza, in date May 15, 1903, is in *Bollettino Emigrazione*, 1903, 14.

the request for indemnification, it would be naïve to expect it would come from the offenders since they will never be known, or, if they are discovered, they probably are workers and agents of the labor unions: people with no money." Even if the request for an indemnification could be pursued, in that moment it wasn't politically viable to "monetize" the "blood price," as demonstrated by the accusations against Minister Prinetti by Senator Fava for the Erwin lynching: "Moreover, in the present case that has some characteristics of a lynching and where there is a victim, I don't know if the intervention of the Royal Embassy would receive approval, after the very recent declarations of Minister Prinetti who rejected, in front of the whole Senate, the shame of having exacted a blood price."[89]

---

[89] ASDMAE, idem. From the Italian Embassy in Washington to MAE. June 29, 1903.

V. WHEN LAW ENFORCEMENT ACTS: NINE POTENTIAL LYNCHINGS THAT DID NOT HAPPEN

1. NEW ORLEANS, LOUISIANA, 1896

On August 26, 1896, in the same state and in the same month of the Hahnville, Louisiana, lynching, Rocco Bonora was arrested in Bayou Goula under the suspicion that he killed an old lady, Ms. Landry, and was under heavy threat of being lynched.[1] But this time the dastardly act didn't take place because law enforcement intervened to prevent the highly probable slaughter. According to the Italian Consul in New Orleans Papini, the tragedy was avoided "thanks to the precautions taken by judiciary authorities of this state."[2] The Italian man was later acquitted of the charges and was set free.[3]

2. MANSURA, LOUISIANA, 1901

One month after the lynching in Erwin, Mississippi, an "incident" took place in Mansura, Louisiana. In reality this was an attempted homicide, even though Consul Papini described it as a "missed lynching" (Mississippi was in his area of pertinence). The reconstruction painted the picture of an Italian family that had reached a moderately successful position as store owners, the only Italian family in town to have done so. Apparently the local population did not appreciate this in the least. Papini in describing the events to the minister of foreign affairs wrote: "A young and industrious boy, 17-years-old Antonio La Nasa, had

---

[1] "Bayou Goula's Bloody Deed. The Mistery of the Murder of Old Ms. Landry," in *The Daily Picayune,* August 28, 1896.
[2] ASDMAE, Serie Politica "P" (1891-1916), b. 623, f. 631. From the Italian Consulate in New Orleans to MAE, August 31, 1896.
[3] ASDMAE, idem, November 4, 1896.

opened a store selling a variety of goods in the town of Mansura. On the side, he also had a job as a cobbler. The growing success of his business triggered the jealousy of several inhabitants of that place and especially of other store owners. On the night of August 17, 1901, his house was targeted by a volley of bullets shot by several firearms that left forty or fifty bullet holes in the walls. The boy and three other young Italians living in the house survived by throwing themselves on the floor. The assailants nailed a sign to his house threatening him with death if he didn't leave the town in four days. He reported the facts to the sheriff, also adding the names of probable suspects. Despite the sheriff's reassurance, the boy decided to sell everything and, before the four days were up, moved to New Orleans where he denounced the events to the Italian consulate. The protest from the consulate to the governor of Louisiana and the latter's reassurance did nothing to inspire confidence that things would be any different than they had been in many other similar circumstances. Reflecting this state of mind Papini wrote: "Unfortunately, from the correspondence it is rather obvious that the authors of the attempted murder and death threats are unknown and cannot be found." Certain that the individual responsible for the attack would never be punished, Papini classified this episode as the outcome of the common practice in the South of getting rid of competition using this method: "The Mansura incident, given the place where it took place and the local meaning of the word 'lynching,' must be regarded as a missed lynching: this is a well known habit, very common in the southern states, where it is used as reprisal against commercial competition." The size of the reprisal was commensurate to the size of commercial success on the part of immigrant ethnic groups. "The fact that the most common victims are Italian has to do with the fact that they are tenacious and obstinate in making inroads everywhere, penetrating into any area they can reach, regardless of danger."

The future perspectives, according to Papini, were destined to get worse, and in fact the number of lynchings seem to get higher day by day. "Lynching is taking more and more the shape of a real social scourge. For some time now, it is very rare that a day goes by without a lynching. [...] These abnormal collective crimes don't seem to upset anymore the moral sentiment of the masses: nobody seems to be willing to rebel against this trend. If things continue this way, lynching may become even more common and go through even more atrocious phases." The risk for Italians was bound to grow: "It won't be a surprise if Italians will become even more frequent victims of lynching, since their number is ever increasing in these states and at the same time they belong to the most despised social class."[4] Ambassador Mayor was skeptical about the possibility of obtaining any reparation by the federal government for the losses incurred by La Nasa with his forced move after the threats. Technically, he had left town voluntarily, since the sheriff had promised protection. Formally there were no irregularities in the judiciary investigation. "The suspects were indicted in front of a grand jury and brought to trial. Here they were acquitted for lack of evidence. The regularity of the process was not appealed."[5]

The young La Nasa went on to open a bar in New Orleans, abandoning the plan to pursue reparation. At this point the embassy considered his case closed.[6]

3. Rocky Springs, Wyoming, 1901

This minor episode consisted of a lynching threat that was immediately defused. However, it happened not long after the Tallulah massacre and for a few weeks it preoccupied the Italian consulate in San Francisco, the Italian embassy in Washington, the governor of Wyoming and the secretary of state. An Italian doctor, Fiorangelo Di Giacomo, was arrested in Cheyenne, Wyoming, on June 1901 and accused of having kidnapped Lizzie Brown for a few days, trying to force her to marry him.

There was immediate danger that the Italian would be dragged out of jail to be lynched. The alarm was sent to the Italian embassy by an-

---

[4] ASDMAE, Serie Politica "P" (1891-1916), b. 682, f. 874. From the Italian Consulate in New Orleans to MAE, August 31,1901.
[5] ASDMAE, idem, December 17, 1901.
[6] ASDMAE, idem, March 26, 1902.

other Italian, Gabriele Colangelo, a watchman of the Union Pacific Railroad Company, who swore on the innocence of the doctor and that the accusations had been blown out of proportion. Ms. Brown said she was threatened with death. According to Colangelo, however, it was just a blackmail scheme and that she would withdraw the charge in exchange for money.[7] After paying a bail of $3,000, Di Giacomo was set free. The diplomatic machinery in the meantime had been started in fear that something ugly may happen as in recent cases of lynching. The embassy gave instructions to the San Francisco consul to investigate. At the same time Ambassador Carignani asked the governor of Wyoming that the accused be protected. After receiving reassurance to this effect by the local authorites, on June 29 he informed the embassy that Di Giacomo was in no danger.[8]

4. New Kensington, Pennsylvania, 1902

This episode was connected to the climate of conflicts between workers favoring a labor strike and those who opposed it. The attempted lynching took place on June 20, 1902, in New Kensington, Pennsylvania. The targets were Domenico Santoro and the brothers Luigi and Antonio Marano, all from Rotula Serra in the province of Avellino. Ambassador Mayor wrote to Minister Prinetti that "the origin of the events is contradictory, with different versions: the American version claims the three Italians provoked a fight; in the Italian version, confirmed by the investigation of the editor of the newspaper *Trinacria* of Pittsburg, they are the victims of aggression."

The second version seemed more credible to the ambassador: it would be indeed strange that to defend themselves the three Italians fired shots at a crowd of over two hundred people, furious at them for working in a mine as replacement laborers ("scabs") during a strike.

---

[7] ASDMAE, Italian Delegation in USA, 1901, b. 103, pos. 137, f. 65. Miscellaneous. From . Colangelo, Cheyenne, Wyoming, to the Italian Embassy in Washington, June 16, 1901.
[8] Correspondence in ASDAME, idem.

Whatever the real dynamics of the events were, either defense or attack, Santoro shot and seriously wounded a young man, Frank James, who at first was feared dead. He was the son of David James, member of the union's "look-out committee" that was trying to stop Italians from working.

According to the Italian version, it was David James who started the assault while his son threatened them with a brick. After the menacing crowd had grown, the Italians fled along the railroad tracks, seeking refuge in the house of another Italian where, surrounded by their pursuers, they were arrested by the police and, with difficulty, brought to jail. As soon as they were put in their cells, the large crowd kept trying to break into the prison with a series of assaults, while outside they had already prepared ropes for the hanging. The police resisted until the evening, supported by some citizens who opposed violence. Fearing that the crowd would win the confrontation, the police decided to move the prisoners by train to Greensburg, to a more secure prison. The plan was to use a back door to exit the local jail. The operation was only half successful. While a huge crowd of 5,000 people was gathering in front of the prison to launch another attack, the police and the prisoners ran into a smaller group. After realizing the new plan, the crowd surrounded the train station. The police led the crowd to believe that the prisoners would be put on the 10:00 pm train. Instead, they placed them in a coach that was able to leave undisturbed. When the leaders realized they had been deceived they organized a small posse to pursue their targets but they could not catch up with the coach. All the Italians were in serious condition and one of them was severely injured.

The conduct of law enforcement in this case was praised by the ambassador. The mayor of New Kensington, due to the lack of police personnel, had deputized sixty armed citizens. Despite the quick intervention, at one point someone managed to slip a noose around the neck of Santoro, who barely managed to escape. "I wanted to report this fact — Mayor wrote — because it shows that the danger of lynching is always present, not only in the southern states but also in places like Pennsylvania, which are usually considered progressive and civilized."[9]

After two months in jail awaiting trial, the defense attorney, Paul Gainther, based his arguments on the right of freedom guaranteed by the U.S. Constitution in matters of labor. He condemned the violent method of the striking workers and their attempts to impose their views on Italian workers who, by the way, barely understood the language and did not know what was going on around them. The lawyer also emphasized the fact that the Italians had reacted after being attacked, and he asked for a complete acquittal.[10] The grand jury acquitted Luigi Marano while Antonio Marano and Domenico Santoro were found guilty of inflicting wounds.[11] Overall, this episode confirmed that when law enforcement officers intervened, even in dire circumstances, and they were not conniving with the lynchers, they could stop the worst kind of acts from happening.

5. Minturn, Colorado, 1903

This was another case where police protection was very effective in preventing the lynching of an Italian under serious threat. According to the reconstruction of the events, on the night of December 31, 1902, in a bar in Minturn, a certain Daniel Wright, totally drunk, started offending Italians, calling them "dagos." At that moment an Italian, Natale Molinaro, entered the bar. Angered by the insults, he shot him in the chest, killing him. Under the threat of immediate lynching, he ran away. He was able to find shelter in the house of Judge Maynard where he remained in hiding until he was moved in secret to the Radcliff prison. The newspaper *Roma*, based in Denver, under the headline "Usual Barbarism" published an alarmed comment: "Popular anger hasn't calmed

---

[9] ASDMAE, Serie Politica "P" (1891-1916), b. 683, f. 882. From the Italian Embassy in Washington to MAE, June 30, 1902.
[10] The synthesis of the closing statement is in "Il processo Marano-Santoro," in *Trinacria*, Pittsburg, 1902.
[11] ASDMAE, idem. From the Italian Embassy in Washington to MAE, September 12, 1902.

down yet. For this reason the Italian Consul, Giuseppe Cuneo, was contacted via telegraph so that he would take necessary measures to prevent the lynching."[12]

Consul Cuneo, confronting the risk that the Italian may be lynched — as announced by the local newspapers — went immediately to the governor of Colorado, asking that he issue an order to Minturn public authorities to give every possible protection to Molinaro. The governor assured him that this would be done. The consul was hopeful that "thanks to prompt action Molinaro will not be lynched and will be treated with justice."[13]

6. MAJESTIC, COLORADO, 1903

In May 1903, in the mining camp of Majestic, Colorado, in Las Animas County, Agostino Maccario, nicknamed "Garibaldi," was threatened with lynching for the murder of Felice Cavallotti. After the news appeared in the newspapers, the Italian embassy immediately contacted the consul in Denver who, in turn, asked the governor of the state for protection for Maccario. The request was granted and Maccario was transferred to a prison in Trinidad, Colorado, while awaiting trial, thus defusing "the danger that, before being transferred, Maccario may be taken away from the authorities, who were too weak to resist against the crowd."[14]

7. HOWELLVILLE, PENNSYLVANIA, 1905

After a couple of years of relative quiet on the lynching front, on March 14, 1905, Riccardo Forte was arrested in Howellville, Pennsylvania, under the accusation that he had killed a young boy and a young girl, children of another Italian, a certain De Luca. The next day the

---

[12] "Solite Barbarie," in *Roma*, Denver, January 3, 1903.

[13] ASDMAE, idem. From the Italian Consulate in Denver to the Italian Embassy in Washington, January 4, 1903. See also G. Cuneo, "L'immigrazione italiana nel Colorado e nell'Utah," in *Bollettino Emigrazione*, 1902, 5.

[14] ASDMAE, idem. From the Italian Embassy in Washington to MAE, June 4, 1903.

Washington Post reported that a lynching of the presumed culprit was a possibility. Ambassador Mayor alerted the Italian consul in Philadelphia urging him to appeal to the governor of the state "to prevent by any means that a second crime will be added to the first one." He also personally alerted the State Department just to add more pressure. According to some commentators, the phenomenon of lynching was connected to the climate. Among them was the ambassador: "As usual, as the nice weather returns, we observe an increase in the lynchings in the states of the Union. The crime allegedly committed by Forte is exactly the kind for which lynching is the most frequently applied punishment."[15]

8. New Orleans, Louisiana, 1907

Walter Lamana, an eight-year-old child, was kidnapped on June 9, 1907. The father, a well-to-do funeral home owner, received a letter from the local Sicilian Mafia, the "Black Hand," with a ransom request of $6,000 for the return of his son. The ransom was not paid. The Italian Consul in New Orleans, Lionello Scelsi, informed Ambassador Mayor of the crime and warned about rumors of lynching, further describing the security measures he had adopted: "Nine Italians arrested and indicted between last night and today. Fearing violence I obtained transfer from police station to central prison, with double guard."

The consul informed Mayor that Italians living in the community immediately organized a "mass meeting" inviting the American population to participate and protest against the criminal act. The goal was to constitute a "vigilance committee" composed of Italians and others to prevent blackmail or crimes by the "Black Hand." The measure by the "healthy" part of the Italian population appeared as a legitimate reaction but in reality it was only a ploy to prevent further acts of violence that could potentially extend to the whole Italian colony — not just the people in prison. The consul interpreted personally the idea of the mass meeting and the vigilance committee as "a shrewd move by the organizers of the demonstration who, as soon as the kidnapping was committed,

---

[15] ASDMAE, idem. From the Italian Embassy in Washington to MAE, March 18, 1903.

understood that the American population was getting frantic in a dangerous way against the colony. With this public protest against a chain of crimes committed by the "Black Hand" they wanted to take cover — and were able to do so — from the rage of the American population." The promoters of the initiative were not at all irreprehensible individuals: "If one reads the list of people on the so-called vigilance committee, one could see that there are several people with no morality and with very well known shady precedents."[16]

The mutilated body of the dead child was found two weeks later. The consul expressed great concern to the embassy about possible repercussions, despite the reassurances from public authorities that had resorted to the use of the militia: "The danger of violence against the accused," the consul wrote, "is still real. Contradictory rumors are circulating. Governor Blanchard took every adequate measure and even called in the militia. If violence will come to pass, it will happen during the transfer of the prisoners from the prison of New Orleans Parish to that of St. Charles Parish where the killing took place and where they will be tried in court."

The methods used to extort confessions in the county prisons were not very orthodox. The rumor that the Italians were receiving a treatment close to torture worried the consul who protested with the mayor: "I heard that some confessions have been extracted by subjecting the prisoners to the so-called 'sweating system,' that consists in suspending the inmate with a rope around his neck, or, in other words, with a short-lasting hanging. I therefore went to New Orleans to see Mayor Behrman to complain that these methods are not compatible with modern civilization and that they cannot be justified even by the goal and legitimate wish to obtain prompt justice against a crime that presents no extenuating circumstances. With the assurance of the mayor that he would not tolerate illegalities, the consul was satisfied that there would be no danger, "also based on a Supreme Court decision that declared that nobody

---

[16] ASDMAE, Italian Consulate in New Orleans to MAE, b.1. fasc. "Mano near." From the Italian Consul in New Orleans to the Italian Embassy in Washington, June15, 1907.

can be condemned on the basis of confessions made under the pressure of physical violence."[17]

The kidnapping and assassination of the child represented the last in a long series of criminal acts inside the Italian colony of New Orleans that had exasperated the population at large. The equation identified Italians with Sicilians and Sicilians with Black Hand mafiosi. The consul wrote to Minister Tittoni: "Unfortunately this is the most sensational in a long series of assassinations, extortions, assaults and arsons committed for vendetta that have gone on for years in this colony where there is a very high number of ex-prisoners and criminals on the run from the Royal authority. These people managed to escape and now here they have formed a vast criminal association that includes several 'above-suspicion' people, namely all of those that in colonial jargon are called the *prominenti*. This shady and turbulent slice of the population is exclusively Sicilian. This segment of the colony showed great attachment to the Mother Land as a decoy to cover illegal activities: at night they commit criminal acts, but in the daylight they organize festivals and parades to celebrate glorious anniversaries of our country."[18]

The final verdict of the trial created commotion: four out of six accused were found guilty but they were spared the death sentence, contrary to the provisions of the law. According to the consul, the verdict was issued under threat: "The jurors, most of whom were farmers, very likely were scared of the Black Hand. Their verdict was absurd: after finding them guilty they did not apply the death penalty." The danger of a lynching immediately grew. "The verdict created deep indignation in Hahnville, the city where the trial took place, and in the surrounding towns. Several lynch mobs were immediately assembled, armed and determined to hang the four culprits."

Maybe the fact that the wound of the New Orleans lynching of 1891 was still open influenced the authorities who did not participate in or cover illegal actions. The consul wrote to Minister Tittoni: "Fortu-

---

[17] ASDMAE, idem From the Italian Consulate in New Orleans to the Italian Embassy in Washington, June 28, 1907.
[18] ASDMAE, idem. From the Consulate in New Orleans to MAE. June 29, 1907.

nately, after I appealed to the governor, he gave me ample assistance. Five militia companies were moved to Hahnville just a few minutes before the lynchers arrived. They pushed back several night-time assaults to the prison to capture the prisoners but they failed." The climate was still tense, the lynchers were not resigned, and Italians were hated even more. "To give a measure of the public sentiment against Italians and in particular the four assassins suffice it to say that the governor in person, on horseback, joined the soldiers that escorted the prisoners from the Baton Rouge station to the penitentiary — the danger of lynching being so great. The soldiers had to make their way through the crowd with the bayonets at the ready, surrounded by the most atrocious insults of *dagoes-lovers* [sic] while women spit on their faces because they were protecting the prisoners from the inevitable lynching."[19] The American press was outraged at the scandal of the verdict. The New Orleans *Daily Picayune* described the verdict as "a miscarriage of Justice."[20]

9. PITTSTON, PENNSYLVANIA, 1908

It was June 15, 1908: during a minor dispute a group of Italians killed an American and severely wounded a second. The two victims were members of the Central Labor Union. The citizenship immediately reacted with threats of lynching. As had already happened in other circumstances, the lynching was avoided because the public authority wasn't complicit or conniving, as Ambassador Mayor wrote to Minister Tittoni: "The public authorities courageously did their job: they sheltered our unfortunate citizens — later found innocent — from the fury of the mob, calling the militia to the defense of the prison and the prisoners."[21]

All Italians, not just the people suspected of the aggression, were at risk of being lynched. The newspaper *L'Indipendente*, published in New

---

[19] ASDMAE, idem. From the Consulate in New Orleans to MAE. June 23, 1907.
[20] "Miscarriage of Justice in St. Charles," in *Daily Picayune,* July 19, 1907.
[21] ASDMAE, Serie Politica "P" (1891-1916), b. 683, f. 882. From the Italian Embassy in Washington MAE, June 23, 1908.

England, printed a large headline the day after the incident: "20 Italians Risk Lynching." The article described some details of the rescue operation, showing the excellent work of the public force in dealing with an overly excited mob that was getting ready for the collective ritual of lynching. "Four of the suspected assassins, the first ones to be arrested, were blocked by a crowd of thousands who prevented the police from taking them to jail. The agents had to engage in a real fight to protect their lives from the rage of a mob determined to lynch them. When the police captured Verazza (one of the suspects) the frantic crowd was four thousand strong. The six policemen could not hold back the drunken mob that managed to grab hold of the prisoner to lynch him. He owes his life to Mayor Gillespie who took him out of the hands of the crowd when he was already out of consciousness" while twenty Italians, arrested and imprisoned as suspects of the homicide, were under protection.[22]

The *Trinacria*, a Philadelphia newspaper, reported about the ferocious climate against Italians: "Summary justice was avoided, but the unlucky fellow suffered such severe wounds that is life was in danger. The mayor's words managed to calm the rage of the mob that remained outside the prison chanting: 'Lynch all the Italians! Death to the dagoes!'" Obviously the tension against Italians remained extremely high and the exasperated population was planning reprisals against the foreigners: "The mental state of this population is extremely excited and the majority wants the Italians thrown out. The Central Labor Union, to which the two victims belonged, reflecting the popular sentiment, has called for a mass meeting for tonight [...] to discuss the present situation and demand more protection from the authorities against the criminal activities of foreigners."[23]

---

[22] "20 Italiani in pericolo di essere linciati," in *The Independent*, June 16, 1908.
[23] "Five Italian killers. The crowd tries to lynch them," in *Trinacria*, June 16, 1908.

VI. THE LAST LYNCHING OF ITALIANS

1. Tampa, Florida, 1910

The last lynching with Italian victims took place in Tampa, Florida. Of course, this abominable practice did not cease to exist, in particular against African Americans, and for decades Italians were still subjected to horrible forms of abuse and maltreatment.

The lynchings as well as cases of *peonage* — namely, the forced detention of workers — in the southern states were not infrequent, as many Italians had already seen.[1] In 1908 Gerolamo Moroni, consular agent for immigration in New Orleans, was sent by the consulate to investigate cases of lynchings or attempted lynchings of Italian subjects in the southern states, which he placed in the context of a progressively wider panorama of social and ethnic conflicts. The description rendered by Moroni in some of these cases, even if they didn't compare to the worst tragedies, gives a larger picture of the kind of discrimination that surrounded Italians and that gave fertile ground to the Tampa lynching of 1910.

Moroni in reporting the results of his inquiry wrote: "First: in Sumrall, Mississippi (October 1, [1907]), attempted lynching of Francesco Scaglione. Second: in Chatamville [sic], Louisiana, mass violence on three workers, one dead and two wounded. [...] At first it seemed that the victims were Italian; however, the investigation revealed that they were Bulgarian. Third: in Kentwood, Louisiana, (February 25, 1908) [we took] action in order to prevent Americans from chasing out of town or from lynching the Italians as they had threatened.

---

[1] "Il peonage nel Sud degli Stati Uniti," Rapporto del R. Addetto all'emigrazione Italiana in Nuova Orleans, Gerolamo Moroni, in *Bollettino Emigrazione*, 1910, 5.

"The causes of these lynchings or lynching attempts are to be found in the economic crisis that generated a reduction of jobs and salaries and, consequently, has induced American workers to fight against the competition from foreign labor. In addition to all these reasons is the antipathy of Americans for foreigners and the lack of preparation by the [hiring] companies and the local authorities."

Another important source of information in Tampa is Consular Agent John Savarese who, in March 1908, sent to Rome his answer to a "request for information" distributed by the Ministry of Foreign Affairs to all consulates, based on a common template.[2] The data collected by Savarese gave an accurate picture of the local colony, composed of approximately 1,600 families for a total of about 7,000 Italians, mostly from Agrigento, Palermo, Catania, Caltanissetta, Siracusa, Messina, Benevento and Avellino. Two-thirds of them worked as cigar makers, others were employed as farm workers, fishermen, barbers, etc.

The largest number of Italians worked in the numerous cigar factories in Tampa. Interesting descriptions were given by Fara Forni and Luigi Villari, who were working for the consulate, after two visits respectively in 1904 and 1907: "In Florida [...] the largest colony is undoubtedly in Tampa, with 3,500 fellow Italians, the greatest majority of whom are Sicilians. Two thousand come from the province of Agrigento, others are from Piana dei Greci and Palermo: there are also a few Neapolitans. Most of them work in the town's 33 cigar factories. The tobacco is imported from the island of Cuba. Tampa's products represent a very strong competition against the real Havana cigars in the entire United States. This is not an easy job to learn: the training lasts from six months to a year, but it takes at least three years to become an expert worker. During the training period, the workers do not receive a salary, indeed in some cases the workers have to pay the company for admission." Although the Sicilian families were extremely traditional and conservative, many women were working in the factories and were in fact sought after for their ability: "The women become very good in that job and there

---

[2] ASDMAE, Diplomatic Delegation in Washington (1848-1901), b. 150.

are cases of young Italian women in Tampa that earn as much as $25 a week. On the average a worker makes between 16 and 18 dollars a week."[3]

The lynching of Angelo Albano and Costanzo Ficarotta in Tampa on the night of September 20, 1910,[4] was investigated by Vice Consul Moroni of the immigration office on instructions by the Italian consul in New Orleans. The inquiry, conducted in a very rigorous manner turns out to be well documented, well argued, credible and of great interest for the complex picture it portrays, confirming in large part the information contained in previous surveys. Moroni calculates that the overall population of Tampa was approximately 50,000 people, composed of Americans, Hispanics, Cubans, Blacks and Italians. The Italians were about 6,000-7,000, mostly Sicilians and most of them employed in the cigar industry. Among the Italian colonies in the United States, Tampa's had one of the worst reputations because of the large presence of common criminals and also organized crime. A long strike in the cigar factories contributed to exacerbating the climate in the city. Moroni explained that "the reasons leading to the lynching are rooted in the serious crimes committed by Italians, especially in the period between 1908 and 1910, which have been left unsolved due to the lack of witnesses. Another cause is the strike of cigar workers who, for the last three months, have gravely damaged the economy of the city. The first reason was the pretext needed to annihilate or defeat the second."

---

[3] "Gli italiani nel distretto consolare di Nuova Orleans," from a report by cav. G. Fara Forni, with contributions by cav. Luigi Villari, consular agent for immigration, in MAE, Commissariato dell'Emigrazione, "Emigrazione e colonie," collection of reports by Royal Diplomatic and Consular Agents, III, "America," Rome, 1909.

[4] Sul linciaggio di Tampa cfr. L. Pilotti, La Serie "Z — Contenzioso" dell'Archivio Storico — Diplomatico del Ministero degli Affari Esteri, "Il Veltro. Rivista della civiltà italiana," n.1-2, gennaio-aprile 1990, pp.105-110; Pozzetta G. E., Italians and the Tampa General Strike of 1910, in Pozzetta G. E. (ed.), Pane e Lavoro. The Italian American Working Class, Toronto 1980, pp.29-46; Ingalls R. P., Urban Vigilantes in the New South: Tampa, 1882- 1936, The University of Tennessee Press, Knoxville, 1988, pp.96-99.

Moroni went on to describe the activities of the Black Hand that, inside the Italian colony, could act undisturbed thanks to the complicity of the so-called Tampa Colony's *prominenti*, who, here just as everywhere else, are the true plague of all our colonies in America." The *prominenti* of the Italian colony in 1908 formed a "Committee of Public Safety" to "uproot the Black Hand from the midst of Italians." Shortly afterwards "the Gentlemen of the Committee started an extra-legal police corps that acted with such hubris that street crime became even worse, bringing even more dishonor to the Italian colony in Tampa. [...] This Association imposed extortions on Italians according to their wealth with threatening anonymous letters. [...] The authorities did nothing to stop it, first of all because it was all happening among Italians, second because they had dirty political motives."

After yet another crime in the Italian colony in 1909, "the local newspaper *The Tampa Morning Tribune* in an editorial warned that if justice could not follow its course, a lynching could take place: the regular justice had never been able to sentence any Italian due to the solidarity, both moral and financial, of the whole community." The reticence or outright refusal to testify during trials was well known but wasn't peculiar of Italians only: "All the crimes committed by Italians or Spanish or Cubans are almost always unpunished because these races do not want to testify. Indeed, they conspire to deceive justice and threaten witnesses. The police are also to blame: they are too corrupt, composed of people appointed by the electors of the county for a period of four years, and therefore under their direct influence and under threat of vendettas."

Moroni also criticized the judiciary system and the impotence of police in front of lawyers whose fees depended on their ability to grant impunity. "All these reasons had as a result that all the crimes were left unsolved and as a consequence popular indignation exploded all at once." In these circumstances there was also a strong interest on the part of some in causing the failure of the cigar makers: "The West Tampa businessmen and manufacturers have seized the opportunity to defeat the strike."[5]

There were plenty of reasons for the strikes in the cigar factories, first of all the awful working conditions. In 1908 Vice-Consul Moroni had already denounced the high toxicity of the work environment: "The workers who produce cigars are often victims of TB, that they incur by working in large heated rooms full of nicotine."[6] But the ultimate cause of the conflict between owners and workers was the refusal to raise salaries. The strike was followed by a shutdown.

Moroni and the rest of the diplomatic and consular personnel almost all belonged exclusively to the aristocracy and they were not at all supportive of the unions (the American Federation of Labor and its affiliate, the Cigar Makers' International). They ascribed great responsibilities to the unions, accusing them of being interested only in increasing membership to increase revenues: "The goal of the International wasn't to take care of the interests of the workers, who were well paid and well treated. It was to push a large portion of the 10 to 13,000 workers who weren't union members to sign up for the unions. The interest was to enlist them to their cause in order to benefit from the monthly dues."

Moroni also accused the union of having caused an economic and social crisis with a strike that had been going on for three months in a city where cigar manufacturing was the main source of income and wealth. "The city of Tampa depends largely on this industry and the strike has reduced its revenues significantly. The population is suffering serious damage, business is down, commerce is at a standstill and as a consequence people are on edge. It takes very little to start a conflict. There are approximately 6,000 or 7,000 workers on strike and many cigar workers left to go to Havana, Key West, New Orleans, Sanford etc. to work in other plants owned by the same companies." As often happens in the case of long, protracted strikes, the relations among workers started deteriorating: "The strikers have gone from quiet protest to visible

---

[5] ASDMAE, idem. "Relazione sul linciaggio di Tampa, Florida," October 5, 1910. From the Italian Consulate in New Orleans to MAE, October 8, 1910.
[6] *Bollettino Emigrazione*, 1908, 16.

action: they started with blocking their workmates from leaving, and now they are interfering with the hiring of scabs (replacement workers). They have thrown stones against trains and finally there was the attempted killing of Joe Cosio, a Spaniard, who was mistakenly identified for his brother who is vice president of the manufacturers' association."

Moroni traced back the steps that led to the people's increased exasperation, focusing in particular on the attempted assassination of J.F. Easterling, accountant of the cigar company Bustillo Brothers & Diaz. "When a committee of the International Union arrived at the factory at the beginning of the strike, Easterling fired some shots in the air to intimidate the workers. Also, he tried to hire replacement workers (scabs) to deal with the strike. Whence the reasons for the attempt against him. Ficarotta and Albano were immediately accused of the crime on the basis of testimonies that, according to Moroni's findings, were not fully credible. "It appears that both Ficarotta and Albano were present when the attempt took place, however, it is not clear to me that they were the authors. [...] In the Italian colony persistent rumors point to a Cuban as the real assassin, someone who had already fled to New York. Ficarotta just happened to stand behind him." Once again the reticence of the Italians blocked the progress of a serious investigation. Discomfited, the vice consul commented: "No Italian stepped forward with the name of the Cuban and nobody wanted to make this extremely important revelation." Although Moroni had determined that the two Italians weren't the shooters, it wasn't enough to clear them completely of the charges. "It's true that the two Italians were not cigar makers themselves and that they didn't have a direct motive to kill Easterling. On the other hand Ficarotta, a bloody killer by trade, might have been hired or instigated by someone else. We should not be surprised if this was the case, given his dark past. It is instead possible that Albano was in that place by pure chance, and, in order to avoid being involved, decided to run around the block on his bike, and this expedient turned out to be his ruin." Moroni also showed how Deputy Sheriff Keaggin lacked clear and incontrovertible witnesses and resorted therefore to fabricating testimonies to frame the two Italians.

The description of the lynching and the plan set in place to actuate it constituted a major accusation against the lynching mob but most of all against the public authorities that did nothing to prevent it, thus implicitly becoming accomplices. Based on Moroni's reconstruction, the episode could not be classified as a sudden outburst of rage by the crowd. Moroni stated that "the lynching plan was prepared in the most minute details by an expert hand, to the point that the local paper, the *Tampa Daily Times* wrote that 'the crowd did a good job.'" After the arrest the two Italians were taken to the city jail: "They were surprised they had been arrested but not worried." The vice-consul insisted that it would be useless to count on spontaneous testimonies and on the investigation by the police. The only credible witness, according to Moroni, "is terrified of the police and does not want to take chances. It's not even worth it to report the official declarations by Deputy Sheriff Evans, or the written statements of fireman Bryan [...] because they are irrelevant: both people were accomplices in the lynching." According to the coach driver who brought the two Italians to the prison, the coach was stopped shortly afterwards by twenty or twenty-five armed people who *speaking perfect English,* ordered him to turn over the prisoners to them." The deputy sheriff did not resist nor protest: he only fired four shots in the air. Everything was staged, including the telephone call to the police and the "farce of the hot pursuit of the assaulters," who passed by the place of the lynching without seeing a thing. Also the supposed suspicions about a group of Spanish or Cubans were a ploy to throw the Italian consul's investigation off track. Finally, the late discovery of the two hanging bodies, at 11:30 pm completed the act. "The operation took place quickly. The location of the hanging had been chosen in advance. The two men were tied back to back. As an act of final derision, someone put a pipe in Ficarotta's mouth. [...] Around Albano's neck a sign read: 'Warning. Everybody watch out from following in the same steps. We know seven more. If other citizens are molested, watch out. Justice.' In the morning around 8 am the ropes were easily untied by the dog-catcher, Mr. Schelman. Others say it was the chief of police who untied them, but these testimonies come from Americans, and cannot be trusted," Moroni commented.

"The seven people who have been threatened with the same treatment could be the following Italians with American citizenship who after the lynching received threatening letters and an eviction order." The message continues with the names of the seven people and their professions. Two of them were "wretched criminals" who had committed crimes both in Italy and in Tampa. Two were involved in the strike: Giovanni Vaccaro "threatened because he was believed to be an agitator, escaped to New York and at present writes newspaper articles against the Italian authorities about the lynching." "Angelo Leto fled to New York: on September 5 he had given a speech in Sulphur Spring, near Tampa, to urge the strikers to resist against the owners."

The role of the local press was immediately supportive of the lynching. All one needs is "the terrible editorial under the headline *A Lynching Lesson*." This article cynically declares that "the people of Tampa with this verdict wanted to show that they will not tolerate murders committed for greed" and added that the two dead "are victims of the public indignation."[7]

Moroni's conclusions left no illusion: "Based on this article, on the fact that the attackers spoke fluent English, and on the statements made by Keaggin, Evans and Logan in front of me and the Royal Consular Agent, I declare with absolute certainty that no Italian was present at the lynching, contrary to the rumor that circulated at the beginning according to which the Tampa Italian colony wanted to get rid of two dangerous individuals. The only person who mentioned that hypothesis was Col. Hugh McFarlane, but the rumor had been spread intentionally in order to cover the real offenders." Moroni in his indictment also analyzed the characteristics of lynching in general as a "state crime": "Lynching is a crime usually committed by the in-power segment of the citizenship or with its approval, always with the silent consensus of the local police. To verify my statement it's sufficient to analyze all the lynchings — or almost all — committed up until now."

---

[7] "A Lynching and a Lesson," in *The Tampa Tribune*, September 22, 1910.

Moroni was hopeful — sarcastically — that in the future the Italians living in the United States would also learn this method: "Lynching is a crime that Italians are not familiar with but maybe some day our immigrants will learn it from the civilized Americans," was his bitter conclusion.

To Moroni, the interests connected to the cigar manufacturing industry and the damage caused by the long strike were the clear causes of the events, together with the need to teach an exemplary lesson that would have the effect of ending the strike and reestablishing the social hierarchical order. "The industrialists, the store owners and the West Tampa police at the order of McFarlane saw that the strike was disastrous for their interests. As the situation was not improving, they began to fear for their lives and concluded that the means at their disposal through the justice system (which they had corrupted) was no longer sufficient to protect them. At that point, they decided to scare the masses with a terrifying lesson. They needed victims." The two Italians were the right people: Ficarotta was a notorious criminal and murderer "hated by the Americans and hated and feared by the Italian colony that he terrorized. His death would be welcomed by all." Albano, a close friend of Ficarotta, had a clean record [...] but he started supporting the strikers and showing up at their meetings. [...] He had clashes with McFarlane over some [money] interests, an area where Americans don't forgive or forget. Albano didn't realize that since he was not American he wasn't strong enough to fight the Don Rodrigos[8] of West Tampa — to his great misfortune."

According to the vice consul the chance of bringing the authors of the lynching to justice was practically nil. "There is no evidence against the citizens of West Tampa both because Italians don't want to talk and the Americans are not going to accuse any of their own. However, the public opinion and the circumstances demonstrate that it was their con-

---

[8] One of the "bad guys" in Alessandro Manzoni's novel *The Bethrothed* (*I promessi sposi*). The novel's characters are by far the best known of the entire Italian canon and have become metaphors, not unlike Shakespeare's most famous characters.

spiracy to get rid of two dangerous subjects and at the same time frighten the striking workers."

Just as certain was Moroni. The involvement of the authorities wasn't limited to allowing the lynching: they actually helped organize it. "There is no doubt that the police, or at least part of it, were in the conspiracy, but, again, evidence is lacking and one can only draw conclusions from the clues. [...] I think we can reasonably deduce from those clues that the police was an accomplice or at least knew about the conspiracy. Even if they had no part at all, they took no measures to protect the lives of the two arrested. Indeed, they handed them over to the attackers without resisting, as if it weren't their duty to protect them. Moreover, it is clear that, up to this day, they haven't done anything to find the culprits."[9]

2. THE EMBASSY REACTS

Immediately after the lynching of Angelo Albano and Costanzo Ficarotta, on the night of September 20, Acting Consul in New Orleans Papini sent a telegram to Ambassador Paolo Montagliari informing him of the event and that other cases of violence were possible. Even more worrisome was the fact that the Italian colony wanted to hold a "mass meeting." The ambassador's answer by telegraph seemed more concerned with the agitation in the colony than with the crime itself: "I urge you to recommend to the colony that they keep a dignified and calm demeanor abstaining from protests that could interfere with the activities of the authorities." He ordered him to send Honorary Vice Consul Moroni to start an investigation. The embassy in turn informed the secretary of state and the governor of Florida, urging them to give protection to the colony and to start "an investigation aimed at finding and punishing the culprits of such a barbaric act." Florida's Governor Albert W. Gilchrist answered the ambassador telling him that, based on his information, the two Italians had already obtained American citizenship —

---

[9] ASDMAE, idem, *Relazione*.

which was actually true for Ficarotta — and that an investigation was under way "regarding last night's unfortunate occurrence."

The ambassador described to Minister of Foreign Affairs Marquis di San Giuliano the seriousness and complexity of the situation, and most of all the possibility that the crime had been planned inside the Italian colony, as the local newspapers were claiming. "Unfortunately we are confronted by an extremely serious event," the ambassador wrote, "something the likes of which has not happened since the Erwin massacre of 1901. The aspect that makes this episode even more painful for us is the possibility that — based on newspapers' reporting — the lynching was perpetrated by Italians, and that the causes may be sectarian issues."

The reconstruction of the socio-economical context of the lynching, based on credible sources, pictures the Italian colony as being split between a few good people and many evil maffiosi [sic]. This helps understanding the dynamics that could have led to the lynching, within the framework delineated by the ambassador. "It seems that the city, known for its cigar factories, enjoys a reputation for peace and order. There lives a rather sizable Italian community, composed primarily of Sicilians. In this colony, as unfortunately happens in many of our colonies, especially in the South, there are two groups: a few people who with entrepreneurship and hard work have reached a relatively prosperous position and enjoy the appreciation and respect of Americans; and another group, a mass of unsavory characters, maffiosi whose main means of support is the extortion of their better-off paesani."

The ambassador initially linked the lynching of September 20 with the murder, the previous autumn, in 1909, of two of the most respected Italians in Tampa, barbarically killed by other Italians. Another link connected the lynching to the workers' strike at the cigar manufacturer Bustillo Brothers & Diaz, the majority of which were Italians and Cubans. Florida, just like several other states in the South, was not unfamiliar with lynching, and not only of black people: "It is rather disquieting that in this country there are repeated acts of this barbarism, whose victims are not only blacks but also whites."[10]

Naturally, the embassy could not act until the issue concerning the nationality of the two victims had been cleared. The next day, on September 23, a message from the ambassador informed Minister di San Giuliano that Ficarotta had become an American citizen while Angelo Albano was still Italian. He also reported that several newspapers questioned the police version that there were several Italians in the lynching party. The embassy immediately filed a protest by the ambassador with the State Department on September 23: "It seems that the local police has not taken sufficient measures to protect the lives of the two arrested who were only suspected of wounding an accountant of the company Bustillo & Diaz. The police agents, instead of trying to defend the two unfortunates while they were shackled, abandoned them to their destiny without making any attempt to block the killers from committing this premeditated crime." The embassy took a very hard stance against "the responsibilities of the local authorities who, in this occasion, have failed to anticipate and also to use force to prevent this misdeed."[11]

Ambassador Montagliari reported to the minister that Count Moroni, who had been sent to Tampa to investigate, had found the situation to be under control. However, "the authorities seem to display maximum inertia in looking for the culprits of the lynching." Further humiliation was inflicted on the community: "Count Moroni found out that there were photos on sale with the images of the lynching. He protested to the mayor asking that the sale be stopped." With regard to the reputation of the victims, he reported that "news yet to be verified claims that the two victims had an awful record and were abject individuals, extortionists, or, to use a word created in this new colonial environment Manoneristi ["Black-Handists.]"

---

[10] The epistolary exchange and the telegrams are in ASDMAE, Serie "Z", Usa, b, 33, f. 27/2. From the Italian Ambassador in Washington to MAE, September 22, 1910.
[11] ASDMAE, idem. From Italian Embassy in Washington to MAE, September 23, 1910.

The colony obviously was up in arms about this crime against Italians. In Montagliari's comments: "The mournful event in Tampa created a very deep impression in the colonial community. The Italian-language newspapers every day print violent articles about it, and every day the embassy receives letters of complaint from associations and private citizens who deplore the event and protest against the action of American authorities."[12]

Moroni's reaction had some positive effects and put an end to the sale of the lynching's photos. "The Governor Stops Sale of Lynching Pictures" was the headline of *The Tampa Daily Times* of September 27, explaining that the measure was adopted after the complaint from the Italian vice consul, with an order by the governor to Sheriff Robert A. Jackson. *The Tampa Morning Tribune* of September 28 tried instead to discredit with new facts at least one of the two Italians, revealing that Angelo Albano had sworn falsely that he was an American citizen, born in New Orleans, while in reality he was born in Italy and still owned an Italian passport. He also registered illegally in 1909 for the elections the following year in the state of Florida.

As soon as the embassy received documentation showing that one of the two victims was an Italian citizen, Ambassador Montagliari, on October 1, sent a note to Secretary of State Philander Knox showing evidence that Angelo Albano was born in Italy "and not, as Florida state authorities claimed, in New Orleans." He repeated the demand that the culprits be found and punished, and denounced the "culpable conduct" of Tampa's police: "Tampa's authorities failed in their duties. I do not intend to accuse them of tacit complicity with the crime, but, with great pain, must resign to the fact […] that the above-mentioned authorities are not making any attempt whatsoever to find the culprit of the murders of September 20; nor do they show any in-tention of wanting to punish them, should they somehow be found."

A copy of Ambassador Montagliari's note to the secretary of state was sent to Minister di San Giuliano along with a report about the ambassa-

---

[12] ASDMAE, idem. From Italian Embassy in Washington to MAE, September 26, 1910.

dor's meeting with Undersecretary of State Alvey Adee who — presumably impressed by Montagliari's accusations — "promised he would act immediately urging the federal 'Attorney' [Attorney General?] to open an inquiry in case the Tampa police were really remiss in the search for the culprits." On the basis of the information received by Moroni, the ambassador was convinced that "the police, anxious to get rid of the dangerous criminal Ficarotta and his subversive friend Albano, were silent accomplices in the murders, and that they now do not care to find the offenders."

However, once it was determined that one of the victims was a foreigner, the federal authorities had the right and duty to act directly and take serious punitive measures, a perspective that was not shared by state authorities. The latter, in fact, insisted that the victims were American citizens so as to let the culprits go unpunished or, if they were found, give them insignificant sentences, similar to an episode "that happened a few days ago, when the authors of a lynching of an American detective in Ohio were sentenced to 20 days in prison,"[13] as the ambassador commented.

The American labor movement took notice of the Tampa lynching since it took place in the context of a strike. The unions wanted to emphasize the connections between the explosion of the social conflict and the ensuing attempt to repress the unions. In reality, the two Italians did not work in the cigar factory, nor were they union activists even though Albano was supportive of striking workers. The socialist press justly remarked that the lynching was used instrumentally to put an end to the long strike. *The Chicago Daily Socialist* of October 4, 1910, linked the alleged unionist activity of the two Italians to their lynching under the headline "Lynching of Union Cigar Men at Tampa," with the gruesome photo of the two hanged Italians. The daily followed with a report about protest demonstrations that took place in various states after the murders: "Protest meetings are scheduled by Italian associations, by unions and by local socialist sections in every corner of the country." The Tam-

---

[13] ASDMAE, idem. From Italian Embassy in Washington to MAE, October 2, 1910.

pa lynching was openly denounced as fitting within a climate of anti-union intimidation. "It is not safe for a union man to walk the streets of Tampa" the newspaper wrote, listing a long series of violent aggressions against local unionists.

The newspaper also printed the press release that had been approved by a group of Italian workers in Chicago "during a meeting of Italian workers of Chicago's 17th district, which is almost exclusively Italian." About the two "union leaders, guilty only of trying to organize the Tampa strikers," the article issues a stern protest "against this brutal act by capitalists assisted by a ferocious police and a mercenary press" but mostly "against the so-called mob law." The same interpretation was given by the anonymous author (probably Max Baginski) of an article that appeared on the magazine *Mother Earth* on the cigar workers' strike: "Two Italian union activists were lynched, the organizers were chased out of the city, the strikers' headquarters were burned down, and everything happened with the secret complicity of the city's authorities."[14]

In such a difficult climate, the grand jury issued its report concluding that the perpetrators could not be found. Vice Consul in New Orleans Papini, greatly demoralized, wrote to Ambassador Luigi Cusani Confalonieri that although it was a foregone conclusion that nobody would be punished, he had hoped that the authorities would at least stage a fake trial against somebody, with an inevitable acquittal for lack of evidence: "On the one hand I didn't expect the culprits would be punished, on the other hand I thought they would bring to trial some of the alleged perpetrators, knowing full well that in the end they would be acquitted. But it is an enormity to close the case with the declaration that it's impossible to find anyone connected to the lynching."

According to Papini, such a scandalous conclusion was made possible in part also by the negligence of the Italian consular agent in Tampa, Saverese. His assessment was supported by the attaché for immigration Moroni and by Ambassador Cusani Confalonieri who filed a reprimand with Minister di San Giuliano. In Papini's words: "If we came to this

---

[14] *Mother Earth*, 1911, 11.

outcome, part of the blame rests with the agent who, in my opinion, neglected his duties and showed very little interest in the issue. This opinion is shared by Count Moroni: Mr. Savarese enjoyed a high social position in Tampa's upper circles[15] and he could have gathered important information to unravel the mystery, if not immediately at the time of the lynching, at least in the aftermath. However, he comported himself deplorably in order to avoid compromising his standing, and by doing so he undermined the investigation of Count Moroni."[16]

Because of the Tampa events of 1910, the protracted economic crisis caused by the cigar makers' strike that lasted seven months, but also the sensation that the lynching had on a national and international level, the Italian population in Florida dropped significantly. In a 1911 report, Vice Consul Moroni wrote: "The total approximate number of Italians resident in Florida was between 7,000 and 8,000 in 1908. During the cigar makers' strike many returned to Italy and others moved elsewhere looking for work. Today we estimate that about 5,000 Italians are left."

The Italian colony in Tampa counted approximately 4,000 people of a total population of 45,000. Its economic situation had worsened considerably although future prospects still seemed bright: "Our fellow nationals were all in excellent condition before the strike, but some were forced to dip into their savings and go into debt in order to survive during the seven-month strike. Their conditions should return to normal now that industrial production of cigars has restarted vigorously." Despite the drop in Italians living in Tampa, the presence of Italian workers was still considerable: "The largest portion, about 3,000, are employed in cigar manufacturing. Before 1908 there were 6,000 Italians out of a total work force of 13,000."[17]

---

[15] According to available records he was a member of City Council from March 1892 to March 1894.

[16] ASDMAE, idem. From Italian Embassy in Washington to MAE, January 28, 1911.

[17] G. Moroni, "L'emigrazione italiana in Florida," in *Bollettino Emigrazione*, 1913, 1.

3. A Predictable Ending: "The Blood Price"

Initially, Ambassador Cusani Confalonieri chose not to submit to the State Department any requests for reparation, preferring to wait until Secretary of State Knox made his proposal "to settle the incident." As a hint, he sent him instead a copy of the letter written by Secretary of State James Blaine to chargé d'affaires in Washington Imperiali after the 1891 lynching, in effect suggesting that he follow that precedent that included a statement deploring the massacre and an indemnification of 125,000 francs by the federal government to the Italian government. Cusani wrote to di San Giuliano: "I told him in friendly terms that I was hoping for a similar settlement, in addition to all the other measures against the dereliction of duty on the part of the local authorities." Cusani Confalonieri, however, was less combative than Ambassador Fava, claiming that the position of the embassy after the Tampa lynching was weaker than in the New Orleans mass lynching. In the case of Tampa the direct responsibility of the local authorities was extremely serious but difficult to prove and that was "the weak spot of our protest in comparison to the New Orleans lynching, when it could be proven directly that the police was at fault."[18]

Cusani Confalonieri again, after the lynching of a Mexican man in Texas on November 3, 1910, considered contacting the Mexican Embassy in Washington: "Since this lynching is analogous in many aspects to the Tampa episode [...] it is clear that our two countries have a common interest in this case." The victim was a Mexican citizen, Antonio Rodriguez, "who, accused of raping and killing an American woman, was captured by a mob, beat up and burned while — it is said — still alive."[19]

The U.S. State Department tried to deny, or admit only partially, its responsibility with a little subterfuge, namely comparing the Tampa lynching to the killing in Italy of two American sailors. Cusani Confalonieri in a letter to di San Giuliano, wrote: "The State Department

---

[18] ASDMAE, idem. From Italian Embassy in Washington to MAE, February 17, 1911.
[19] ASDMAE, idem. From Italian Embassy in Washington to MAE, November 12, 1911.

seems well disposed toward the solution of the Tampa lynching: in a message to the governor of Florida it stigmatizes implicitly the conduct of the local authorities and notices the need to give satisfaction to the complaint. However, in a rather strange shift, it compares the Tampa misdeed to the killing and wounding of two American sailors in Catania on October 24, 1909." Cusani Confalonieri asked for more information on this incident but at the same time excluded that there could an "exchange" over the two cases: "In general terms, I shall notice that a comparison between the Tampa and Catania cases is not admissible, since in Catania the incident happened in the course of a brawl."

Faced with the accusation of negligence put forth by the State Department against Catania's authorities, Cusani Confalonieri did not know enough about the case to rebut the federal government's claim: "Even if we allowed for the most unfavorable hypothesis in this case, it seems to me we should never accept a specious link between the two cases, which are completely different." The ambassador's consistency apparently had some effect, at least in separating completely the two cases. On the Tampa case, though, he seemed willing to close the case with the usual "charity," and was indifferent whether the money should come from the federal government or the state of Florida: "If that state were to offer an indemnification, in my opinion we could consider the issue of material damage satisfactorily closed. We don't care which authority pays up, as long as the indemnification is actually paid. There is a risk that the State Department will try to hide behind the refusal of the state of Florida. In that case we will need to remind them that the indemnification for the New Orleans lynching was not paid by the state of Florida but by the Federal Government."[20]

As usual, it took a long time for the reparation to be paid out: over two years later, on June 26, 1913, President Woodrow Wilson recommended that Congress vote in favor of an indemnification of $6,000 for the lynching of Angelo Albano. The president, as in other analogous cases, recommended the allocation "as an act of grace and without reference

---

[20] ASDMAE, idem. From Italian Embassy in Washington to MAE, March 2, 1911.

to the question of liability of the United States." The text of the resolution submitted by Secretary of State William Bryan on June 24, 1913, recommended that Congress approve the allocation without even implicitly hinting at possible negligence on the part of Florida's authorities, or to the scandalous verdict against unknowns. The text, however, mentioned other cases of lynching of Italians, in Walsenburg, Hahnville, Tallulah and Erwing, declaring that the Italian government "had requested an indemnity of $6,000."[21] The debate in Congress about the indemnity and its amount was particularly heated: some objected that the family of Angelo Albano — who, incidentally, never expressed any desire to become an American citizen — would receive benefits that were not available to American citizens. How Congress would end up voting was still an open question. Cusani Confalonieri in a message to di San Giuliano wrote: "I noticed that the issue of the amount hasn't even come up for debate yet and I expect that it will be the main objection. In fact, the average amounts of previous indemnities awarded to Italy and other States is around $2,000. I insisted on the higher amount of $6,000 using as leverage the delay by the previous administration in starting the procedure. I do expect there will be problems with this issue."[22] The House of Representatives, after a long and heated discussion, approved the indemnity of $6,000. Cusani Confalonieri could not hide his satisfaction for what he considered a personal "victory," since he was able to triple the usual award.

The ambassador directed all the consuls in the United States to publicize this "success" in all the Italian communities to counter the unrelenting complaints against the embassy's weakness, especially in the case of lynchings, which never led to the punishment of the culprits, and were always closed with the usual "charity money." In his message to the consuls he wrote: "It is my policy to avoid any form of favorable publicity for this Royal Embassy, which is only performing its duty. However, I will defer to your personal decision whether to publicize to Italian citi-

---

[21] *Message from the President of the United States,* June 26, 1913, House of Representatives, 63rd Congress, 1st Session, Document No. 105, in FRUS 1913, pp. 619-20.
[22] ASDMAE, idem. From Italian Embassy in Washington to MAE, September 8, 1911.

zens the outcome of this case, thus making a positive impression on them and reassure them about the protection given to them by the Royal Government. In case you should decide to do so, I would prefer that the colonial press talked exclusively about the steadfast action of the Royal Government, without mentioning in any way this Embassy."[23]

The decision to publicize the amount without mentioning that, once again, the Italian government had been unable to receive justice, did have some results: the Chicago-based newspaper *L'Italia* on November 25, 1913, came out with the following headline: "Italian Government's Stunning Victory in Favor of the Mother of Man Lynched in Tampa, Fla." The article stated: "Our country's Government gave proof of its industry and zeal in the defense of the interests of an Italian citizen."

---

[23] ASDMAE, idem. From Italian Embassy in Washington to all the Consuls in the United States, November 20, 1913.

VII. AMERICA INTERROGATES ITSELF

1. The "Fava Solution"

After being appointed to the Senate, former Ambassador Fava remained involved in the juridical and political issues surrounding the lynching of Italians. In an essay written in 1902, during the dispute about the Erwin, Mississippi, massacre of 1901, the senator took stock of the situation and discussed the central question at the base of the contention between Italy and the United States. The core issue was "the important juridical and constitutional issue whether the Congress of the United States may, or may not, send to the federal courts crimes of lynching of foreigners; and if real and true federal courts exist in all the individual States of the Union."[1]

According to Fava the answer to the second question was affirmative, despite the objections of "illustrious statesmen." To support his claim, Fava pointed to the fact that the Supreme Court, located in Washington, oversaw the work of nine federal circuit courts whose decisions were valid for the entire country. Each one of the circuits was headed by one of the Supreme Court justices, with jurisdiction over crimes that involved a violation of federal statutes.

Senator Fava was trying to reconcile the irreconcilable, drafting the outline of a compromise that would not be offensive or otherwise curtail the powers of the individual states, but that at the same time would allow the federal government to respect international treaties. "Concerning the alleged impossibility for Congress to refer to the District Courts the jurisdiction over crimes of foreigners' lynching, this power may already exist *de facto*. However, Congress has the right to refer this legisla-

---

[1] F.S. Fava, "I linciaggi agli Stati Uniti. La questione giuridica," in *Nuova Antologia*, 1902,

tion to federal magistrates, as strenuously argued by Senator Foräker, proponent of the bill whose purpose was to 'assure the punishment of the violations of the rights of foreigners stipulated by treaties.' In an attached report submitted to the U.S. Senate on February 14, 1900, that state-of-facts — that is arguably anti-juridical — was rectified by the unanimous consensus of the Senate Judiciary Committee."

Fava attributed the source of the bill to his initiatives. "In my parliamentary question of December 20 in the [Italian] Senate to the Honorable Minister of Foreign Affairs, I reminded him that the [U.S. Senate] bill was the result of long, non-official but friendly negotiations that I started in 1899, immediately after the Tallulah episode, initially with the late President McKinley and later with the Chairmen of the House and Senate Committees in charge." Concerning the agreement that led to the bills, Fava claimed that they "placed within the purview of the federal courts the authority to decide cases of lynching of foreigners since they are federal crimes. The bills, thus, reconcile the prerogatives of the laws and courts of the individual states with the inviolable duties of the federal government, freely subscribed in solemn treaties which, after being ratified by the legislative branch, became *ipso jure* federal laws."

Fava continued: "We heard the objection that a highly respected number of American statesmen, such as Webster, Evarts and Blaine, were resolute in opposing any change to state laws in our direction. They openly endorsed the doctrine whereby the only guarantee affirmed by the treaties for the protection of foreigners is complete equality of treatment with American citizens in the different states of the Union. But these were their arguments when the episodes of lynching of foreigners were not as frequent as they became later, and when experience had not yet taught that in these cases the local prejudice makes it impossible to obtain justice in state courts. After several cases of lynching of foreigners remained unsolved, the federal government felt the need to take the jurisdiction over these crimes away from the local courts and from local prejudices."

This was the goal of two presidents, Harrison and McKinley, who in their messages urged Congress to approve the bills presented by Senator

Davis and Congressman Hitt, two valiant advocates of international laws. The Senate Committee also worked in this direction, as per the statements by Senator Foräker. Fava commented: "All these initiatives tend to implement the concept that every crime committed in any state against a foreign citizen constitutes a violation of federal laws and, as such, must be adjudicated by federal courts *according to the laws of the specific state*. This last concession was meant to satisfy the jurisdictional rights of each individual state."[2]

Fava was implicitly critical of Minister Prinetti who, in his opinion, did not apply enough pressure on the American institutions in the Erwin case to arrive at the result that seemed within reach after Fava had prepared the terrain. At the same time he was hoping that his report would work as a "stimulus to our government for additional steps in the future." The problem did not concern only Italian citizens but all foreigners, the aliens and their governments: "My work consisted in prodding the legislative branch to affirm the responsibility of the national government. This would benefit all foreign citizens resident in the United States and they would be in debt to Italy for this initiative."

The present phase of stall was interpreted optimistically by Fava who thought it would be only temporary and constituted nevertheless the starting point for future negotiations with the federal government. The report continued: "If for some new circumstances the bill so strenuously supported by Senator Foräker should not be debated by Congress, it will not cease to be the framework for new negotiations, particularly after the new massacre in Erwin."

In reality the situation did not allow for much optimism. Secretary of State Hay forwarded to Congress the Italian protest after the Erwin massacre. However, the new president, Theodore Roosevelt, as we previously saw, did not react to the pressure and in fact his message to Congress did not mention this issue at all. Minister Prinetti had dodged Fava's question in the Italian parliament: "Do you hope to be able to have the new Congress reexamine bills similar to those introduced in

---

[2] An analysis of Senator Foräker's bill is in Pierantoni, *I linciaggi negli Stati Uniti*, pp. 45-6.

1900?" Ignored by Prinetti, Fava insisted: "Why this silence? It makes one almost fear that the issue has lost ground and that the Italian protest is going to be archived somewhere on Congress's shelves. And yet the path I opened up is the right one and there is reason to believe that if we pursued it in the same cautious but determined way, we would reach our goal easily, since it now enjoys the support of illustrious American thinkers."

Despite all this, the path opened by Fava was not pursued by Prinetti nor by any of his successors at the Ministry of Foreign Affairs. The Constitution of the United States was never modified in the part that concerned the relation between the federal government and the individual states. And to conclude, the legitimate needs of our government, weak and in need of an outlet for millions of emigrants, never received satisfaction.

2. Plans without Results

Between the end of the nineteenth century and the beginning of the twentieth, the American public opinion, the press and all other institutions, confronted with the steady increasing number of lynchings, began a heated debate on the topic. Even some of the states that had never before experienced this plague started recording episodes of summary justice, and this pushed Congress to look for a solution at the federal level. In the House session of May 26, 1902, New Hampshire Senator Gallinger introduced a motion to charge the Senate Judiciary Committee with an investigation on the matter and to recommend possible institutional solutions. The senator asked for unanimous approval. Since lynching was generally considered a crime typical of the South, he preventively explained that it wasn't his intention to raise a regional question. He presented statistics that showed numerous cases of lynching had taken place also in northern states and that some of the victims were white, although, of course, the great majority were black. The problem, thus, concerned the entire country. Many in the United States began to lament the fact that the federal government did not have the power to intervene in the internal legislation of individual states in cases of lynching. The increase in the number of lynchings and the spreading of the phenomenon to a progressively larger number of states demonstrated the fallacy of the argument that, according to some, it was the residue of backwardness and that was the reason why it was more frequent in the South. The statistics presented by Senator Gallinger showed that just in 1901 there were 135 lynchings, not a very high number in comparison to other periods, such as 1892, when there were 235 lynchings. According to the same statistics the "score" for individual states, in 1901, was: Mississippi 16; Alabama 15; Louisiana 15; Georgia 14; Tennessee 12; Texas 16; Florida 7; Kentucky 7; California 6; Missouri 6; Arkansas 2; Virginia 2; Idaho, Indiana, North Carolina, West Virginia, Arizona 1, for a total of 135 cases. Of the total, 121 took place in the South and 14 in the North. The victims were 107 blacks, 26 whites, 1 Indian and 1 Chinese. The crimes allegedly committed by the victims were: homicide 39; assault and rape 19; theft and robbery 12; attempted murder 9; assault and attempted rape 9; attempted assault with the intent of murder 8; horse or cattle rustling 7; money disputes 6; arson 4; suspected homicide 3; suspected assault and rape 1; insult to a white woman 1; suspected theft 1; racial prejudice 9.

The crimes that led to lynchings in many cases did not seem to be only the extremely serious ones. Ambassador Mayor fully agreed in this assessment with Gallinger: "Senator Gallinger noticed that assault cases, that for someone may be a legitimate reason for reprisal by lynching, did not cause many crimes of this kind. Lynching, instead, in many cases is triggered by less serious crimes, and it is often associated with tortures and other outrages that surpass any imagination."[3]

Senator Gallinger's proposal to create a Senate investigation commission did not find much support. He did not get the unanimity needed for immediate action: indeed the resolution did not even get to a vote and was simply added to the Senate agenda. The problems concerned very directly Italians resident in the United States, given the repeated

---

[3] ASDMAE, Serie "P" (1891-1916), b, 683. From the Italian Ambassador in Washington to MAE, May 27, 1902.

episodes of violence against them. The Italian government as well was monitoring with great interest the work of Senator Gallinger, in hopes that one way or another a constitutional change could finally be achieved. In a letter to Minister Prinetti, Ambassador Mayor wrote: "I should mention that the approach taken by Senator Gallinger is the best possible for the interests of our citizens in the regions where lynchings occur. Senator Gallinger is trying to establish that the local justice system is inadequate to the task of judging mob crimes and that these must be referred to the federal justice. This is exactly what we would like to see happen." The ambassador explained that if a constitutional modification had come as a result of pressure by a part of the American public opinion and legislators, there would be no cause to argue that the Italian government had interfered improperly in the internal affairs of a sovereign nation: "Our wish was to achieve this result without being accused of interference in the federal legislation, as someone complained in the past."[4]

President Theodore Roosevelt in a speech at Arlington Cemetery on May 31, 1902, on what would later become Memorial Day, commemorating the soldiers who died in the Civil War, launched into a harsh condemnation of lynching in the United States, without however mentioning the lynching of foreigners. "From time to time in our country there are, to the deep and lasting shame of our people, lynchings carried on under circumstances of inhuman cruelty and barbarity infinitely worse than any that has ever been committed by our troops in the Philippines; worse to the victims, and far more brutalizing to those guilty of it. The men who fail to condemn these lynchings, and yet clamor about what has been done in the Philippines, are indeed guilty of neglecting the beam in their own eye while taunting their brother about the mote in his."[5]

---

[4] Ibidem. See also "La statistica dei linciaggi," in *Bollettino della Sera,* New York, October 24-25, 1901.

[5] The text of Roosevelt's speech on Memorial Day, May 31, 1902 is in ASDMAE, idem. From the Italian Ambassador in Washington to MAE, June 2, 1902.

Despite some hopeful signs at the institutional level that a revision of the Constitution may be possible, the opposition was sufficiently strong to prevent the kind of modifications sought by the Italian government. Ambassador Mayor, quite disappointed, wrote to Minister Prinetti: "I want to make you aware that there is a long road ahead before this people's conscience becomes aware of the moral and juridical enormity of those crimes. I must report that Senator Hoar, Chairman of the Senate Judiciary Committee, who is personally in favor or the resolution, had to report to the Senate that the Committee had tabled indefinitely the proposal." The representatives of southern states were joined in their opposition by others from different parts of the country also firmly against any federal interference that would limit their autonomy. Continuing in his letter, the ambassador complained: "Representative Richardson from Alabama in a speech in the House dared reprimand President Roosevelt for mentioning the crime of lynching in his speech in Arlington. With scornful and ironic tone he accused him of trying to inject the federal authorities in the criminal jurisprudence of the states, and qualified this attempt as inopportune, unjust and hopeless."[6]

Beyond the institutional debate, as we saw the phenomenon of lynching was spreading, targeting mostly African Americans. Ambassador Mayor sent to Minister Prinetti a detailed, precise and articulate analysis of the popular consensus that surrounded this practice and the difficulty, if not outright impossibility, of pursuing the malefactors: "Not a week goes by that in some place in this country without an evil act of lynching taking place. Generally the victims are black people, guilty, or just suspected of some kind of crime against white people. The newspapers report these episodes in the daily chronicles. Whatever inquiry takes place — usually just as a formality — normally does not produce any result because nobody who lives in a place where more or less everyone was involved, will ever testify. So the story is buried and the crime — that remains alive only in the memory — is added to the very long list of similar acts that the chronicles record." Mayor did not

---

[6] ASDMAE, idem. From the Italian Ambassador in Washington to MAE, June 8, 1902.

believe that the "gallows culture" of the southern states was the main cause of the high percentage of lynchings in that part of the country. Rather, he attributed the cause to racial discrimination, which hit harder where the black population was higher: "It is a common belief that lynching is a crime typical of the South and, as a matter of statistics, indeed they are more frequent in this region. But the reason for the higher frequency is probably to be found in the fact that black people — the ordinary victims of mob violence — are more numerous in the South than in the North."

The ambassador reckoned that the practice of lynching was shared not only by those who concretely implemented it, but also by those who should have stopped it, first of all public authorities: "The instincts and passions that cause this social crime are such that to the perpetrators it appears as a form of summary 'justice' and not a felony; and they are identical from one end of the Union to the other. The frequency of the crime's increase does not raise much sensation, let alone disgust, but just sterile and isolated protests. It doesn't even trigger adequate legislative countermeasures. All this means that these passions and instincts are understood and to some extent shared by the same people who should take action."

According to Mayor, a "bestial instinct" is not the only agent that pushes lynchers to commit their crimes, since even "educated and civilized individuals" justify them. Moreover, the lack of certainty of punishment provides a sort of moral alibi: the lynchers were acting to prevent that the offenders may "escape the punishment of legal justice." With reference to a lynching that took place a week earlier in "civilized" Virginia, the ambassador remarked that the mechanisms and the outcomes of the lurid ritual were the same in every state: "The newspapers print long columns full of descriptions and a few lines of commentary. Almost certainly, like in cases where Italians were involved, the investigation will be closed for lack of evidence and, if the magistrate in charge adheres to strict orthodoxy, he will add a few sentences mentioning that the will of God has been fulfilled."

Obviously, the aspect that most concerned the ambassador was the involvement of foreigners and in particular of Italians, given the ambiguous interpretation — restrictive or extensive — that could be applied to the 1871 treaty between Italy and the United States. "As long as this concerns only American citizens, the disregard toward a national crime by the legislative power — albeit willfully complicit — would not touch us much, since every people chooses its own rules. The worst part for us is that, based on the 1871 treaty between Italy and the United States, according to some interpretations, the United States are not required to afford to our citizens a higher protection than is afforded to their own citizens."

The highest federal authorities, even when they express regret and a willingness to engage, did not offer much hope: "I don't think Secretary of State Hay and the president himself share this restrictive view. Indeed, Mr. Hay told me explicitly a number of times that the Federal Authority does not have the necessary power to enforce the existing treaties with regard to the protection of foreign citizens. A contrary position is held by the very influential Senator Henry Cabot Lodge, intimate friend of the president, and rumored to be the next successor of Secretary Hay. He maintains that foreigners are not owed any more protection than American citizens. Others think that referring to the federal justice the jurisdiction of certain crimes that involve the violation of treaties would be akin to a mutilation of the rights of states and, consequently, a violation of the Constitution. They also remind everyone that for a similar reason, the South started the insurrection that led to the Civil War."[7]

The pessimistic outlook of Ambassador Mayor was not without cause. Almost a year after the previous report, there had been no progress. The difficulties or impossibility of modifying the American Constitution were confirmed in a telegram to Minister Prinetti anticipating possible complications in the relations between the two governments: "Let's not delude ourselves. In the future, as in the past, bills against lynching will be introduced. Whatever form they take they constitute

---

[7] ASDMAE, idem. From the Italian Ambassador in Washington to MAE, August 4, 1902.

interference of the federal power in the states' legislations and they will never be approved. For something similar the United States fought for four years in the Civil War. Nobody wants to expose the country to the risk of new conflicts. Moreover, there is the objection that the law guarantees that Italians will receive equal protection with the American citizens, but no more. Every year approximately 150 lynchings of Americans take place."

If lynchings of Italians continue, any initiative by the Italian government would be useless if not outright detrimental for it would be interpreted as a Mafia attempt to infiltrate the institutions of the United States: "Considering that the matter concerns internal affairs, any interference by our part would be rejected. We would trigger a reaction since the Americans already complain that the Mafia has spread its tentacles all the way to this country. Presently the only preventive action against lynchings is the continuous attention of Royal Agents and the request of appropriate responses by the federal and local authorities whenever there are signs of dangerous agitation against our citizens."[8]

For the new Minister of Foreign Affairs Morin, Ambassador Mayor wrote a very caustic analysis of the contradictions of Americans, at the same time a most civilized and a most primitive people: "The Americans who want to bring civilization to the Hawaiians, the Samoans, the Filipinos, and protest against atrocities in Bessarabia, are the same who, every day, show cruel intolerance toward the people of their own country who, according to the Constitution, are endowed with the very same rights — conquered at the cost of a bloody civil war — enjoyed by the very perpetrators of violent excesses." Of course there was a minority sternly opposed to the practice of lynching — and they should not be bunched with the others — but they were totally impotent: "The better people of this country disapprove and condemn. But the reasons of the best are taking too long to penetrate into the great masses, and, frankly,

---

[8] ASDMAE, idem. From the Italian Ambassador in Washington to MAE, May 5, 1902.

the increasing number of lynchings makes us doubt that they will ever penetrate."[9]

The number of lynchings was in fact increasing along with the number of states where they were occurring. In Delaware, for instance, where no previous cases had been recorded, in June 1903 a black man was lynched — and so far everything seemed "normal." Mayor, however, commented that this specific crime was marred "by a unique ferociousness and unanimity of hatred." According to Mayor "this confirms what we have observed for some time, namely that the region infested with the crime of lynching is spreading rather than shrinking."[10] Minister Morin received a new report a couple of months later with new alarming information about the spreading of lynching, with hypotheses about its effect at the institutional level as well as for the American public opinion: "The seriousness of the phenomenon finally struck a chord in the Americans who don't seem to be aware of the shame of the enormity of such barbaric practice. The debate finally started. Statesmen, writers, psychologists, jurists and politicians are denouncing loudly the insanity of these outbursts of crowd rage and the responsible for this new 'weapon of social protection.'" The situation was so alarming that President Roosevelt felt the need to intervene: "The president became aware of the gravity of the situation and he felt the duty to condemn openly the lynchers and the denigrators of the black race, using for this purpose an unusual method, which, because it was unusual, turned out to be even more effective. [...] However, the president won't be able to go further and take more radical initiatives. Nor can he apply pressure on individual states to change their laws, nor would Congress follow him on this path."

It was inevitable to recall the only president who, under the pressure of Ambassador Fava, tried to change the Constitution: "You certainly remember what happened to the initiative of President McKinley who

---

[9] ASDMAE, idem. From the Italian Ambassador in Washington to MAE, June 12, 1902.
[10] ASDMAE, idem. From the Italian Ambassador in Washington to MAE, June 25, 1902.

wanted to make changes in the legislation so that the federal government would have the right to intervene in the investigation and prosecution of lynchers, in any state of the Union." According to the embassy the new attempt by President Roosevelt was also destined to fail: "The presidential message to Congress will certainly fan the flames of acrimony. It is legitimate to doubt that it will bear fruit in practical terms."[11] Even the seasonal ebb and flow of the frequency of lynchings could be observed. Mayor wrote to Minister Tittoni: "Every year in the summer we see a recrudescence in lynchings." About a case that took place in Georgia in which nine men had been murdered — eight black and one white — the social tensions were such that they advised against directing a new influx of Italian immigrants toward that region: "The persistence of these two kinds of crimes, lynching and 'peonage' [...] must make us cautious in advising immigrants about relocating to this area."[12]

The issue of state power versus federal power returned a few years later, in 1909, in the inaugural message of President William Taft. Speaking about the obligations of international treaties, he brought to the attention of the public the need to give more power to the federal authorities thus reducing to some extent state autonomy. Ambassador Mayor was still pessimistic. In a letter to Minister Tittoni he reckoned that "a true solution would undermine the foundations of the Union and would raise protests both in the West and the South. Everything will continue as it did before, with some tweaking."[13] Once again he was right: the following year, in September 1909, the lynching of two Italians in Tampa ended up like all the other cases with the concession of a humiliating indemnity to the families of the victim.

The debate about the rights of foreigners in cases of lynching, however, was to continue for a long time, with new proposals of constitutional

---

[11] ASDMAE, idem. From the Italian Ambassador in Washington to MAE, August 12, 1902.

[12] ASDMAE, Serie "P" (1891-1916), b, 718. From the Italian Ambassador in Washington to MAE, June 30, 1905.

[13] ASDMAE, idem. From the Italian Ambassador in Washington to MAE, March 31, 1909.

reform. President Taft, once again, in a pointed and articulate way, put the problem on the table, refuting one by one all the arguments of those who opposed the role of the federal government in state legislation, using juridical and political arguments of great weight and might. Referring to lynchings of foreigners, primarily Italians and Chinese, along the arc of American history from 1811 to 1910, Taft listed the previous attempts of constitutional reform that began after the New Orleans episode of 1891. In his realistic and disconsolate conclusions, Taft mentioned the small or nonexistent political relevance of foreigners: they were not determinant in electoral terms, therefore they had no influence against the opposition by the states to any constitutional reform.[14]

But this battle, like all the other ones, ended up in a defeat. The crime of lynching, both for foreign and American citizens, never became a federal crime.

---

[14] See W.H. Taft, *Aliens and their Treaty Rights,* in *Antilynching*, Hearings before the Committee on the Judiciary, House of Representatives, 66th Congress, Second Session on H.R. 259, 4123 and 11873. Serial No. 14, January 29, 1920, Government Print Office, Washington, 1920, pp. 14-22.

Index of Proper Names

Abbagnato, Antonio 50
Albano, Angelo 149, 152, 153, 155, 156, 158, 159, 160, 164, 165
Andino, Lorenzo 83, 89
Angelone, Giovanni 133
Angelone, Vincenzo 133
Arata, Daniele 81, 82, 83
Arena, Salvatore 91, 96, 97

Baccelli, Alfredo 24, 126, 127, 128
Baginski, Max 161
Barrilis, Diego 37, 38, 39, 40
Behrman, Martin 143
Bianchi, (?) 79
Blaine, James 51, 52, 53, 59, 60, 65, 68, 69, 70, 163, 168
Blanc, Alberto 37
Blanchard, Newton 143
Bonora, Rocco 94, 135
Brown, Lizzie 137, 138
Bruni Grimaldi, Nicola 82
Bryan, (?) 153
Bryan, William Jennings 164
Butera, Giuseppe 112, 114
Buzzotta, Giuseppe 130, 131

Cabot Lodge, Henry 175
Cabrini, Francesca 18, 54
Carignani, Francesco 29, 114, 116, 117, 119, 120, 138
Carretta, Donato 7
Caruso, Girolamo 50

Cascio, Francesco 111, 112
Cerami, Giovanni 98, 110
Chaffe, W.H. 62
Cirmeni, Benedetto 24, 29, 126, 127, 128, 129
Cleveland, Grover 24
Colangelo, Gabriele 137, 138
Comitis, Loreto 49
Corte, Pasquale 48, 50, 51, 56, 57, 62, 63, 64, 66
Cosio, Joe 152
Cravasso, Antonio 44, 45
Creole 96, 97
Crispi, Francesco 22, 23, 59, 86
Cuneo, Giuseppe 87, 89, 140, 141
Cusani Confalonieri, Luigi 30, 161, 162, 163, 164, 165

Davis, Cushman 33, 106, 109, 110, 122, 168
De Luca, (?) 141
De Riseis, Giovanni 5, 82, 83
Delfina, Giuseppe 103, 104, 105, 106, 111
Di Giacomo, Fiorangelo 137, 138
Di Martino, Giorgio 73
Difatta, Carlo 98
Difatta, Francesco 98, 104
Difatta, Giuseppe 98, 101, 104, 110
Dolph, Joseph 33, 71

Easterling, J.F. 152
Espenard, Robert 91
Evans 153, 154

Fara Forni, Giacomo 148, 149
Fava, Saverio 12, 22, 29, 30, 32, 33, 34, 43, 48, 49, 51, 52, 53, 54, 55, 58, 59, 60, 68, 69, 70, 71, 78, 79, 82, 84, 86, 87, 88, 92, 93, 94, 95, 96, 104, 105, 106, 107, 108, 109, 110, 111, 121, 123, 124, 128, 134, 163, 167, 168, 169, 170, 177
Ficarotta, Costanzo 149, 152, 153, 155, 156, 158, 159
Fiducia, Rosario 98
Foraker, Joseph 167, 169
Forte, Riccardo 141, 142

Gainther, Paul 140
Gallinger, Jacob 34, 170, 171, 172
Gambera, Giacomo 18, 54
Geraci, Rocco 49
Giacobini, Pietro 83, 84, 87,
Giglio, Vincenzo 112, 114, 115
Gilchrist, Albert 156
Gillespie, William 146
Giolitti, Giovanni 22, 23
Gobbetto, Antonio 83, 84
Grimando, Antonio 49
Gueymard, Jules 91, 95

Hanna (see Hollow)
Harrison, Benjamin 70, 78, 85, 168

Hay, John 32, 33, 99, 107, 109, 111, 125, 126, 169, 175
Hennessy, David 50, 57, 72
Hill, David 116, 121
Hitt, Robert 33, 105, 106, 107, 109, 110, 121, 122, 168
Hixon, Abner 83
Hoar, George 173
Hodges 98
Hollow 112, 115

Imperiali, Guglielmo 12, 31, 59, 65, 66, 67, 68, 69, 70, 162
Jackson, Robert 159
James, David 139
James, Frank 138
Janssens, Francis 54

Keaggin, James 152, 154
Knox, Philander 159, 162

La Nasa, Antonio 135, 137
Lamana, Walter 142
Leto, Angelo 154
Liberto, Rosario 112, 115
Liberto, Salvatore 111, 115, 118, 128
Lo Monaco, Alfonso 71
Logan, Marshall 154
Lynch, Charles 3

Maccario, Agostino 141
Marano, Antonio 138, 140
Marano, Luigi 138, 140
Marchese, Antonino 49
Maynard, Judge 140

Mayor de Planches, Edmondo x, 8, 12, 25, 72, 121, 125, 130, 131, 132, 137, 138, 139, 141, 142, 145, 171, 172, 173, 174, 175, 176, 177, 178
McFarlane, Hugh 154, 155
McKinley, William 31, 33, 105, 108, 109, 122, 168, 177
Molinaro, Natale 140, 141
Monaco, Luigi 37
Monastero, Pietro 50
Montagliari, Paolo 156, 158, 159
Moreci, Vincenzo 73
Morgan, John 71
Morin, Enrico 10, 176, 177
Moroni, Gerolamo 7, 15, 16, 76, 147, 149, 150, 151, 152, 153, 154, 155, 156, 158, 159, 161, 162
Motta, Riccardo 56, 57

Nelson 77
Nicholls, Francis 48
Norwood, G.W. 44

Olney, Richard 94, 96, 97
Orsolini, John 78

Papini, Carlo 25, 27, 51, 92, 96, 100, 115, 118, 119, 130, 135, 136, 156, 161
Piazza, Natale 41, 42, 99, 100, 101, 111, 118
Polizza, Emanuele 49
Porter, Albert 23, 59, 64, 65, 66, 67

Prinetti, Giulio 9, 28, 29, 30, 116, 117, 118, 119, 120, 121, 123, 124, 125, 126, 128, 131, 134, 138, 169, 170, 172, 173, 175

Richardson, William 173
Riva, Giovanni Paolo 45, 55
Robilant di, Carlo Felice 43
Roccina (see Roxino)
Rodriguez, Antonio 163
Rogers, George 51
Ronchietto, Francesco 83, 86
Roosevelt, Franklin D. 36
Roosevelt, Theodore 31, 33, 122, 123, 125, 169, 172, 173, 177
Roxino, Joaqiun 91, 94, 96
Rudinì di, Antonio 12, 23, 49, 52, 54, 58, 59, 60, 63, 64, 65, 66, 69, 70

Sacco, Nicola vii
Saint Martin, Giuseppe 72
Salardino, Lorenzo 91, 94, 95, 96
Santoro, Domenico 138, 139, 140
Savarese, John 148, 161
Scaglione, Francesco 147
Scala, Luigi 17, 73, 74, 75, 76, Scalfidi, Antonio 50
Scelsi, Lionello 142
Schelman 153
Serio, Giovanni 111, 112, 114, 115, 128
Serio, Vincenzo 111, 112, 115, 128

Speranza, Gino 18, 129, 130, 133

Taft, William 35, 178, 179
Tirelli, Adelmo 112, 113, 118
Tironi, John 44
Tittoni, Tommaso 8, 25, 144, 145, 178
Traina, Vincenzo 50
Twain, Mark 8

Umberto I 60, 109,

Vaccaro, Giovanni 154
Vanzetti, Bartolomeo vii
Venturella, Giuseppe 91, 96, 97
Verazza, Antonio 146
Villari, Luigi 148, 149
Villarosa, Federico (alias Fransco Valoto) 41, 42, 43
Villere, Gabriel 51
Vinci, Giulio Cesare 99, 101, 103
Visconti Venosta, Emilio 103, 105, 109, 121, 122, 123
Vittone, Stanislao 83, 86

Wilson, Woodrow 164
Woodall, Conrad 88, 89
Wright, Daniel 140

About the Author

PATRIZIA SALVETTI is Associate Professor of Contemporary History at the University of Rome "La Sapienza." She is also part of the doctoral program, "Society, Politics, and Institutions in Contemporary Times," at the University of Cassino. She is past president and current member of the executive committee of IRSIFAR (Roman Institute of the History of Italy from Fascism to the Resistance). She is also a meber of Sissco (Italian Society for the Study of Contemporary History), concentrating initially on the history of the Italian Communitt Party and subsequently on Italian emigration, having received various fellowships for research in the United States and Latin America.

Salvetti's books include: *La stampa comunista da Gramsci a Togliatti* (1975); *Immagine nazionale ed emigrazione nella Società "Dante Alighieri"* (1995); *Guatemala, nascita di una dipendenza (1871-1898)* (2001); *Storie di ordinaria xenofobia. L'emigrazione italiana nel sud est della Francia fra Ottocento e Novecento* (2008); *L'amore al tempo del fascio* (2014); *Oltre-mare. Memorie femminili tra antiche radici e nuove identità* (2016).

About the Translator

FABIO GIRELLI-CARASI is Professor of Italian at Brooklyn College, CUNY. His areas of scholarly interest include the following: Foreign language acquisition, theories and practice; Italian American studies; Holocaust literature; 20th-century Italian literature, in particular Primo Levi and Cesare Pavese. His books include: *Guida all'università Americana* (1997); *Lavorare stanca, canzoniere suo malgrado* (2000); *A scuola con Internet* (2003); *Globalization: Tech-nology, Literacy & Curriculum* (2009).

Most recently, he has completed a translation of Giuseppe Prezzolini's *I trapiantati*, due out in 2017 as *The Transplants*, with Bordighera Press.

SAGGISTICA

Taking its name from the Italian—which means essays, essay writing, or nonfiction—*Saggisitca* is a referred book series dedicated to the study of all topics and cultural productions that fall under what we might consider that larger umbrella of all things Italian and Italian/American.

Vito Zagarrio
The "Un-Happy Ending": Re-viewing The Cinema of Frank Capra. 2011. ISBN 978-1-59954-005-4. Volume 1.
Paolo A. Giordano, Editor
The Hyphenate Writer and The Legacy of Exile. 2010. ISBN 978-1-59954-007-8. Volume 2.
Dennis Barone
America / Trattabili. 2011. ISBN 978-1-59954-018-4. Volume 3.
Fred L. Gardaphè
The Art of Reading Italian Americana. 2011. ISBN 978-1-59954-019-1. Volume 4.
Anthony Julian Tamburri
Re-viewing Italian Americana: Generalities and Specificities on Cinema. 2011. ISBN 978-1-59954-020-7. Volume 5.
Sheryl Lynn Postman
An Italian Writer's Journey through American Realities: Giose Rimanelli's English Novels. "The most tormented decade of America: the 60s" ISBN 978-1-59954-034-4. Volume 6.
Luigi Fontanella
Migrating Words: Italian Writers in the United States. 2012. ISBN 978-1-59954-041-2. Volume 7.
Peter Covino & Dennis Barone, Editors
Essays on Italian American Literature and Culture. 2012. ISBN 978-1-59954-035-1. Volume 8.
Gianfranco Viesti
Italy at the Crossroads. 2012. ISBN 978-1-59954-071-9. Volume 9.
Peter Carravetta, Editor
Discourse Boundary Creation (LOGOS TOPOS POIESIS): A Festschrift in Honor of Paolo Valesio. ISBN 978-1-59954-036-8. Volume 10.
Antonio Vitti and Anthony Julian Tamburri, Editors
Europe, Italy, and the Mediterranean. ISBN 978-1-59954-073-3. Volume 11.
Vincenzo Scotti
Pax Mafiosa or War: Twenty Years after the Palermo Massacres. 2012. ISBN 978-1-59954-074-0. Volume 12.

Anthony Julian Tamburri, Editor
   Meditations on Identity. Meditazioni su identità. ISBN 978-1-59954-082-5. Volume 13.
Peter Carravetta, Editor
   Theater of the Mind, Stage of History. A Festschrift in Honor of Mario Mignone. ISBN 978-1-59954-083-2. Volume 14.
Lorenzo Del Boca
   Italy's Lies. Debunking History's Lies So That Italy Might Become A "Normal Country". ISBN 978-1-59954-084-9. Volume 15.
George Guida
   Spectacles of Themselves. Essays in Italian American Popular Culture and Literature. ISBN 978-1-59954-090-0. Volume 16.
Antonio Vitti and Anthony Julian Tamburri, Editors
   Mare Nostrum: prospettive di un dialogo tra alterità e mediterraneità. ISBN 978-1-59954-100-6. Volume 17.

CPSIA information can be obtained
at www.ICGtesting.com
Printed in the USA
BVOW04s0814200417
481168BV00005B/6/P